AIRCRAFT ARCHIVE

POST-WAR JETS

VOLUME 3

Argus Books Limited
Wolsey House
Wolsey Road
Hemel Hempstead
Herts. HP2 4SS
England

First published by Argus Books 1988

© In this Collection Argus Books 1988

ISBN 0 85242 967 3

Designed by Little Oak Studios
Phototypesetting by Typesetters (Birmingham) Ltd
Printed and bound in Great Britain at the University Printing House, Oxford

Cover photo: Charles E. Brown (R.A.F. Museum Collection)

Contents

De Havilland DH 108	6
Saunders-Roe SRA/1	12
Mikoyan/Gurevich MiG-15 (Fagot)	17
Douglas D.558 Skyrocket	20
Gloster Meteor F Mk 8	22
De Havilland Vampire T Mk 11	24
Douglas F4D-1 Skyray	28
Supermarine Type 541	30
Vickers Valiant B Mk 1	32
Sud-Aviation SO4050 Vautour	36
Supermarine Type 525	38
Boeing B-47E Stratojet	40
Douglas XA4D-1 Skyhawk	44
Armstrong-Whitworth Meteor NF Mk 14	48
De Havilland Comet 1 and 4B	50
Avro Vulcan B Mks 1 and 2	56
Saunders-Roe SR53	68
Mikoyan/Gurevich MiG-21F and PF (Fishbed-C and -D)	70
Vickers VC10 C Mk 1	74
BAC TSR2	82
McDonnell Douglas F-15A and B Eagle	90

A DETAILED COLLECTION OF ORIGINAL SCALE AIRCRAFT DRAWINGS

Introduction

This third volume covering Post-War Jets complements those which ranged over the exciting period of early supersonic fighters and revolutionary shapes. In Volume 1, one can find the French Griffon, American Starfire and British Boulton Paul P.111 alongside the Canberra, Thunderstreak, Super Sabre and Sukhoi Su-7 'Fitter'. On the 'heavy' side, the Victor bomber represented new aerodynamic approaches, contrasted with the Lightning, Starfighter and Draken.

For Volume 2, there was an emphasis on the cleanliness of prototypes in comparison with eventual active-service production versions. The smooth F-86 Sabre, Baroudeur and Leduc were milestones of aeronautical form. The twenty-two subjects in Volume 2 ranged from the Jet Provost trainer, which could be called the only 'conventional' type in the book, to the deltas, swing-wings and VTOL designs which have made plane-watching such a fascinating subject to follow.

Now, in Volume 3, we record more prototypes, intermixed with a few aircraft which have gone into large scale production as, for example, the MiG-21, surely the most widely used jet fighter yet created. One can compare the early adventure of the DH 108 Swallow, a most beautiful aeroplane by any standard of judgement, with the current F-15 Eagle. Was there ever a more challenging task than to design a flying boat fighter? The Saunders Roe SRA/1 proved the specification to be possible. Better known types – the Meteor, Comet, Vampire and Skyhawk – are mixed with Swift prototype, Stratojet and Skyrocket. For detail and supreme accuracy in research, study Dr J F Henderson's drawings of the Vulcans, while, as a monument to a political disaster, Barrie Hygate's TSR2 records an engineering achievement which was cast on the scrap heap by a sad error of Government judgement but is thankfully not oblivious.

For the modeller, the student of aircraft shapes and the collector, this archive of post-war jets is a tribute to the manufacturers – and the draughtsmen who pieced together the accurate outlines.

Each drawing is a typical example of the skill and dedication applied by an amateur researcher over countless hours of translating measurements and photographic interpretation into a scale drawing which, in fact, no manufacturer could ever provide! For it may come as a surprise, but the reality is that the manufacturer's general arrangement drawings have

First-generation British military jets: from the front, a Vampire NF.10 and Meteors F.8, T.7 and NF.11. Versions of the Vampire and Meteor appear as drawings in this volume. ▶

A Stratojet of Strategic Air Command – setting new standards in bomber aircraft in the 1950s. ▶

Pioneering jet aircraft like the DH 108 provided indispensable data during the exploration of high-speed flight in the years following World War II. Plans for this important machine are provided in these pages. ▼

▲
Representing current fighter aircraft in this volume is McDonnell Douglas's potent F-15 Eagle.

little value in the factories, are rarely accurate in shape or scale and, without exception, illustrate the aeroplane in a stage long since superseded by production variants.

Access to the real thing is the ideal, but how can one measure each panel, check every angle and record all the shapes? It takes a special sort of dedication to undertake such a mammoth task. A museum visit will confirm the enormity of the undertaking.

Demand for accuracy and authenticity originated through the work of James Hay Stevens in 'Aeromodeller'. He was among the first to adopt 1/72nd scale, based on the imperial measure of one sixth of an inch representing one foot. Opening standards, as set by James Stevens, were taken up through the series of *Aircraft of the Fighting Powers* volumes published by Harborough, once an associated company with MAP. Wartime urgency quickly generated a new breed of detail draughtsman, typified by Harry Cooper and Owen Thetford. After seven volumes and the creation of an *Aircraft Described* series in Aeromodeller, centred on civil aircraft by Eddie Riding, 1/72nd scale was firmly established, and the fine detail in the drawings reached levels of intricacy to satisfy the most demanding enthusiast – though not for long! Aeromodellers have an insatiable appetite for scale information.

From the immediate postwar years to the present day, the levels of minutiae have soared far beyond the first conceptions. Out of *Aircraft Described* came *Aeroplanes in Outline* and *Famous Biplanes* and, through forty years of publication in 'Aeromodeller' magazine, a band of skilled contributors built up a series which now comes in book form.

The drawings reflect the individual character of the originator. Each was in its time a labour of love, the fruits of which have been the immense pleasure given to students, collectors and aeromodellers. If by reproduction in this form we commemorate their work permanently, rather than in a transient monthly magazine, then we will have rewarded both the draughtsmen and the reader with a treasure store.

De Havilland DH 108

Country of origin: Great Britain.
Type: Single-seat, land-based research aircraft.
Dimensions: Wing span 39ft 0in *11.89m*; length 26ft 9½in *8.17m*; wing area 306 sq ft *28.43m²*.
Powerplant: One De Havilland Goblin II turbojet of 3000lb *1361kg* static thrust or one De Havilland Ghost turbojet of 5000lb *2269kg* static thrust.

Performance: Maximum speed (Goblin II) over 600mph *970kph*, (Ghost) 675mph *1085kph*.
Armament: None.
Service: First flight 15 May 1946.

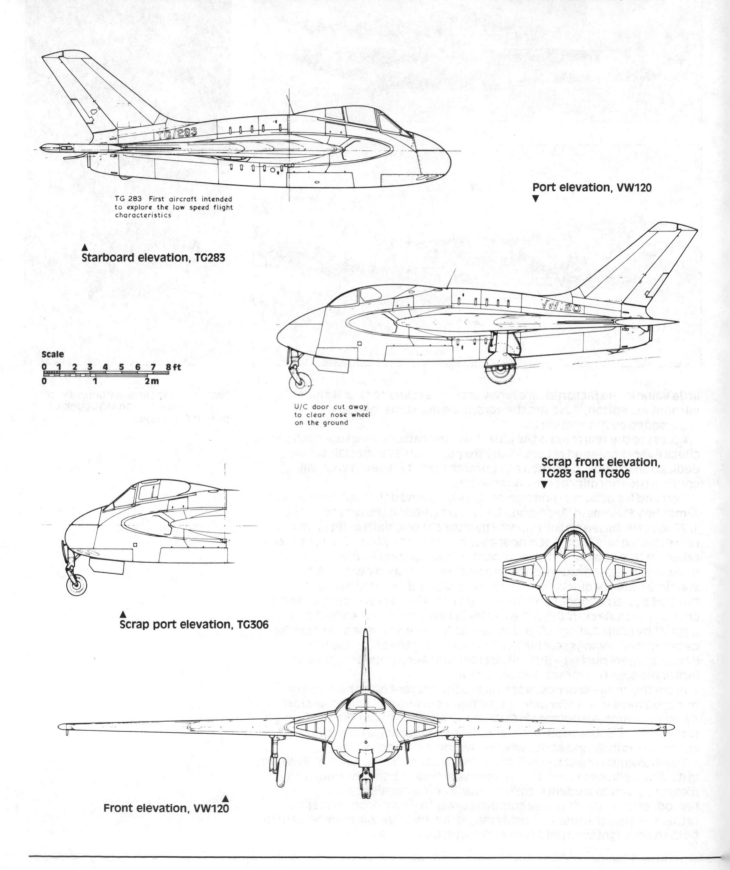

TG 283 First aircraft intended to explore the low speed flight characteristics

▲ **Starboard elevation, TG283**

Port elevation, VW120
▼

Scale
0 1 2 3 4 5 6 7 8 ft
0   1   2 m

U/C door cut away to clear nose wheel on the ground

Scrap front elevation, TG283 and TG306
▼

▲ **Scrap port elevation, TG306**

▲ **Front elevation, VW120**

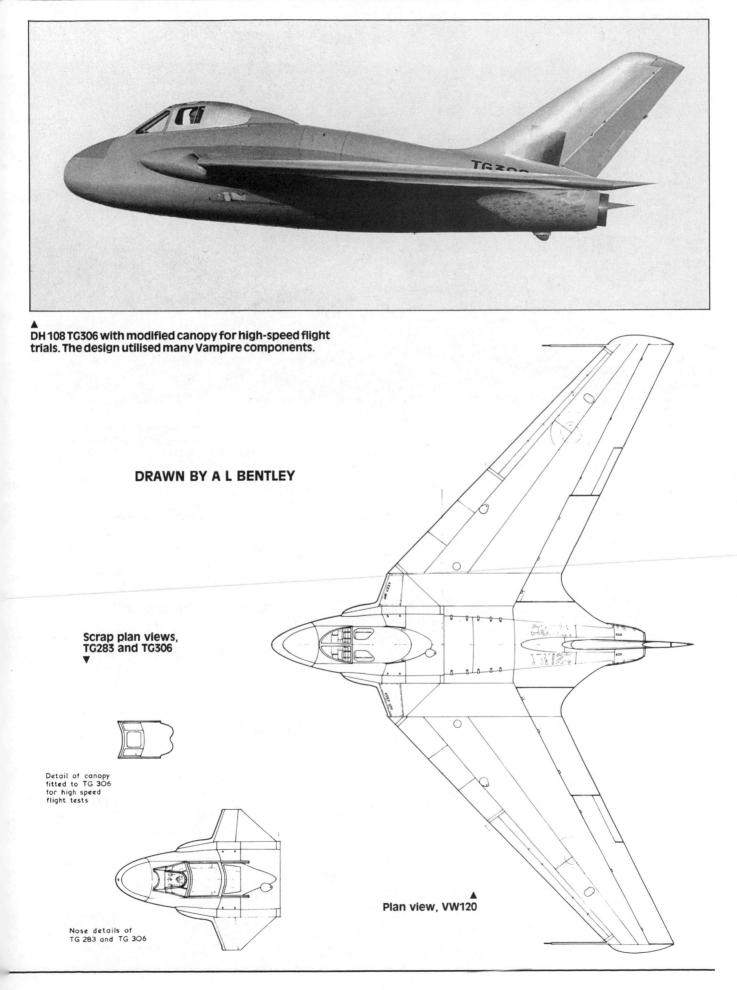

DH 108 TG306 with modified canopy for high-speed flight trials. The design utilised many Vampire components.

DRAWN BY A L BENTLEY

Scrap plan views,
TG283 and TG306
▼

Detail of canopy
fitted to TG 306
for high speed
flight tests

Nose details of
TG 283 and TG 306

Plan view, VW120

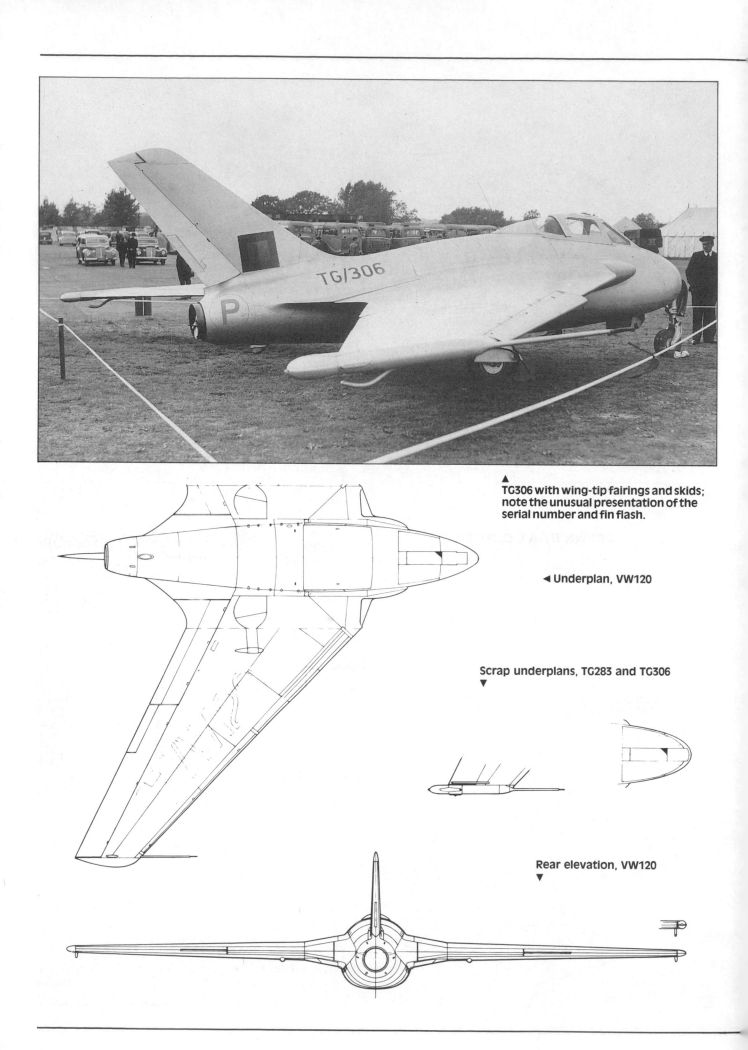

TG306 with wing-tip fairings and skids; note the unusual presentation of the serial number and fin flash.

◀ Underplan, VW120

Scrap underplans, TG283 and TG306
▼

Rear elevation, VW120
▼

Canopy in open position

2a 3a

◄ Inboard profile, TG283

2°
Downthrust

Straight sided cone

Circular sections symetrical about thrustline

Standard Vampire fuselage modified
to suit swept wings

Inboard profile, VW120 ►

1 2 3 4 5 6 7

14

Internal view of high speed aircraft
showing details of ejector seat, high
speed canopy, and revised nose cone

One of the first photographs to be
released of the DH 108, dated 3 May 1946.
The aircraft took only seven months to
build. TG283 was used to investigate
low-speed characteristics of the design.
▼

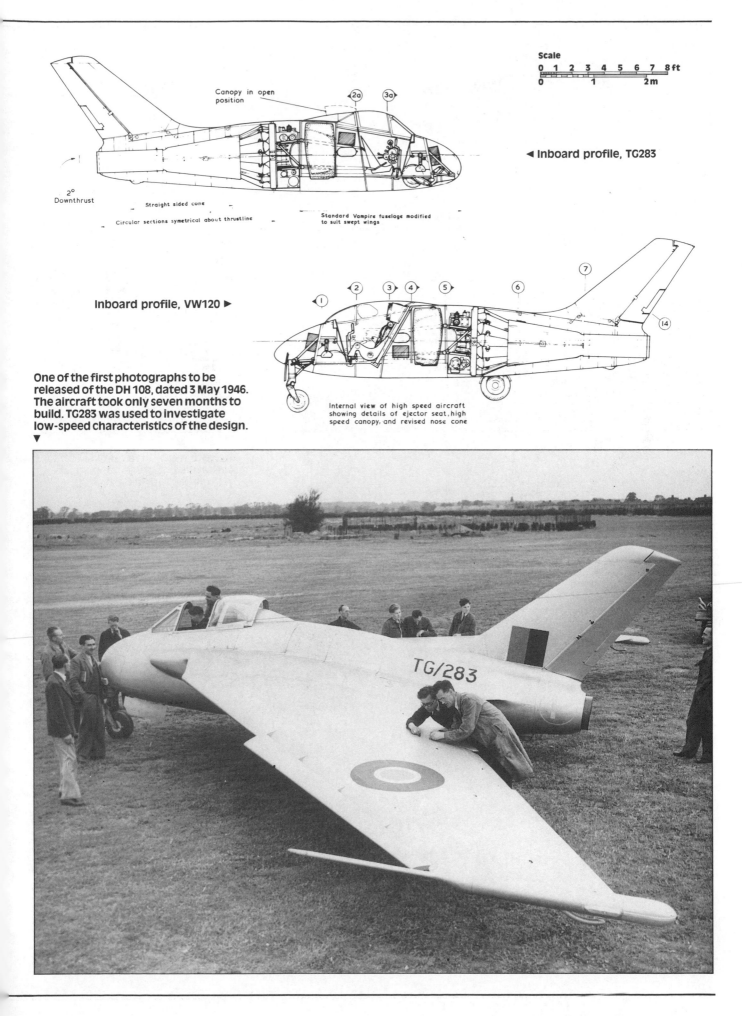

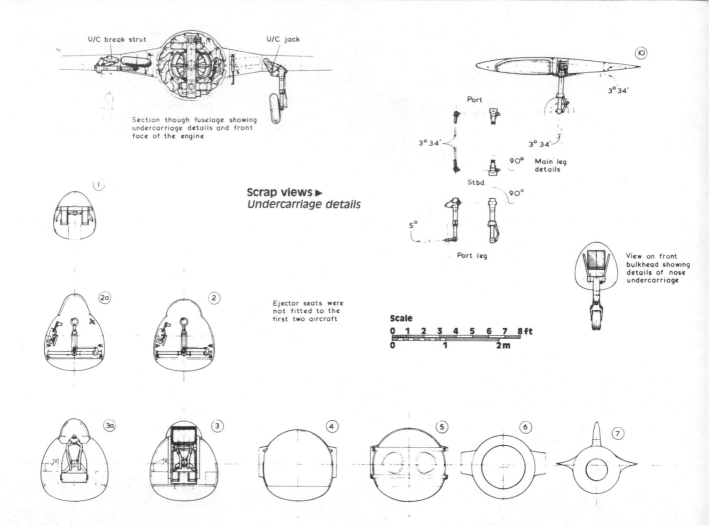

U/C break strut

U/C jack

Section though fuselage showing undercarriage details and front face of the engine

Scrap views ▶
Undercarriage details

Port

3° 34'

3° 34'

90° Main leg details

Stbd.

90°

5°

Port leg

10

3° 34'

View on front bulkhead showing details of nose undercarriage

①

②a ②

Ejector seats were not fitted to the first two aircraft

Scale

0 1 2 3 4 5 6 7 8 ft

0   1   2 m

③a ③ ④ ⑤ ⑥ ⑦

On 27 September 1946, just prior to an attempt on the world air speed record, TG306 disintegrated in mid-air, killing test pilot Geoffrey de Havilland.
▼

▲
Fuselage cross-sections

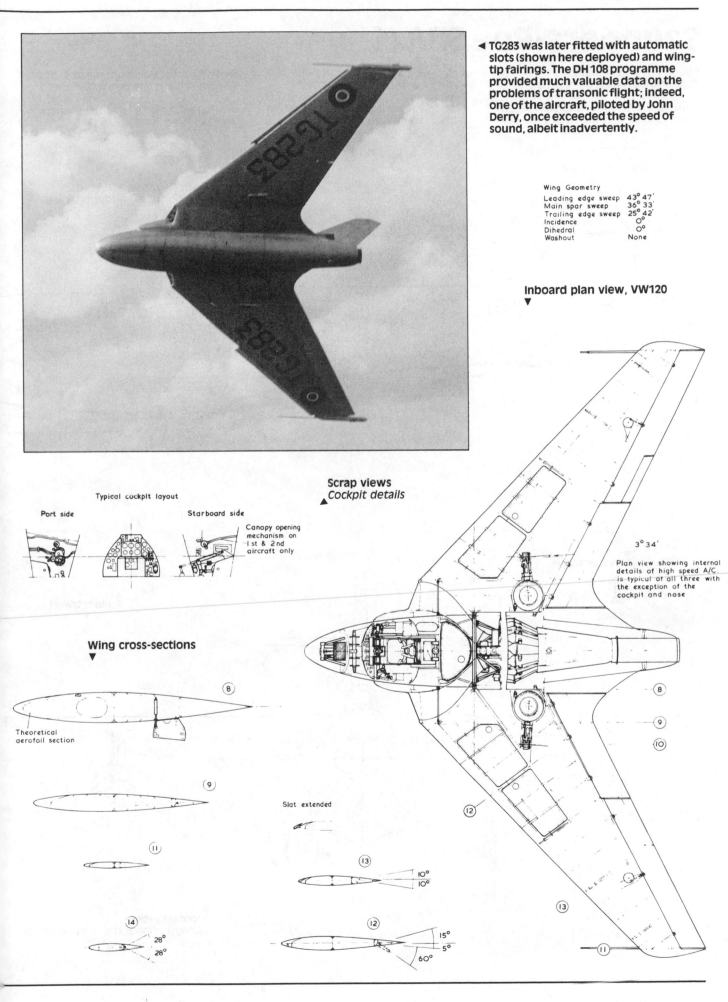

◄ TG283 was later fitted with automatic slots (shown here deployed) and wing-tip fairings. The DH 108 programme provided much valuable data on the problems of transonic flight; indeed, one of the aircraft, piloted by John Derry, once exceeded the speed of sound, albeit inadvertently.

Wing Geometry
Leading edge sweep 43° 47'
Main spar sweep   36° 33'
Trailing edge sweep 25° 42'
Incidence   0°
Dihedral   0°
Washout   None

Inboard plan view, VW120
▼

Scrap views
Cockpit details
▲

Typical cockpit layout

Port side   Starboard side

Canopy opening mechanism on 1st & 2nd aircraft only

3° 34'

Plan view showing internal details of high speed A/C is typical of all three with the exception of the cockpit and nose

Wing cross-sections
▼

Theoretical aerofoil section

⑧

⑨

⑪

Slat extended

⑬   10°
        10°

⑭ 28°
    28°

⑫   15°
     5°
  60°

⑧

⑨

⑩

⑫

⑬

⑪

11

Saunders-Roe SRA/1

Country of origin: Great Britain.
Type: Prototype single-seat fighter flying boat.
Dimensions: Wing span 46ft 0in *14.02m*; length 50ft 0in *15.24m*; height 16ft 9in

5.11m; wing area 415 sq ft *38.55m²*.
Weights: Loaded 16,255lb *7372kg*.
Powerplant: Two Metropolitan-Vickers F2/4 axial-flow turbojets each of 3300lb *1497kg* (later 3850lb *1746kg*) thrust.

Performance: Maximum speed 512mph *824kph*; initial climb rate 4000ft/min *1220m/min*.
Armament: Four fixed 20mm cannon.
Service: First flight 16 July 1947.

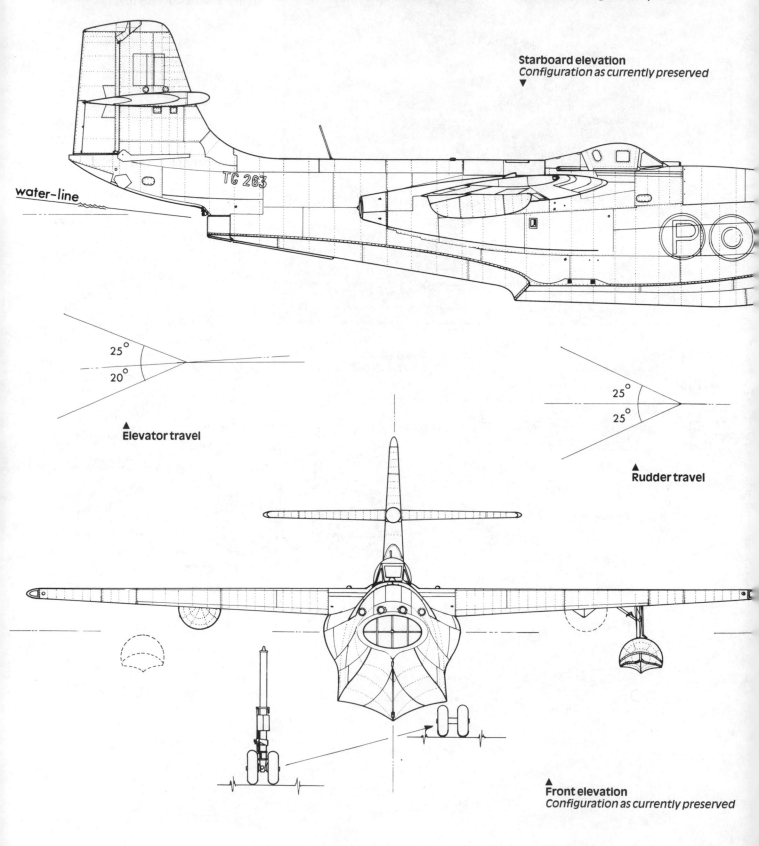

water-line

Starboard elevation
Configuration as currently preserved
▼

TG 263

25°
20°

▲
Elevator travel

25°
25°

▲
Rudder travel

▲
Front elevation
Configuration as currently preserved

Main drawings show configuration applicable to first and second prototypes

DRAWN BY B HYGATE

First prototype: TG263
Second prototype: TG267
Third prototype: TG271

Scale

Plan view
Configuration as currently preserved
▼

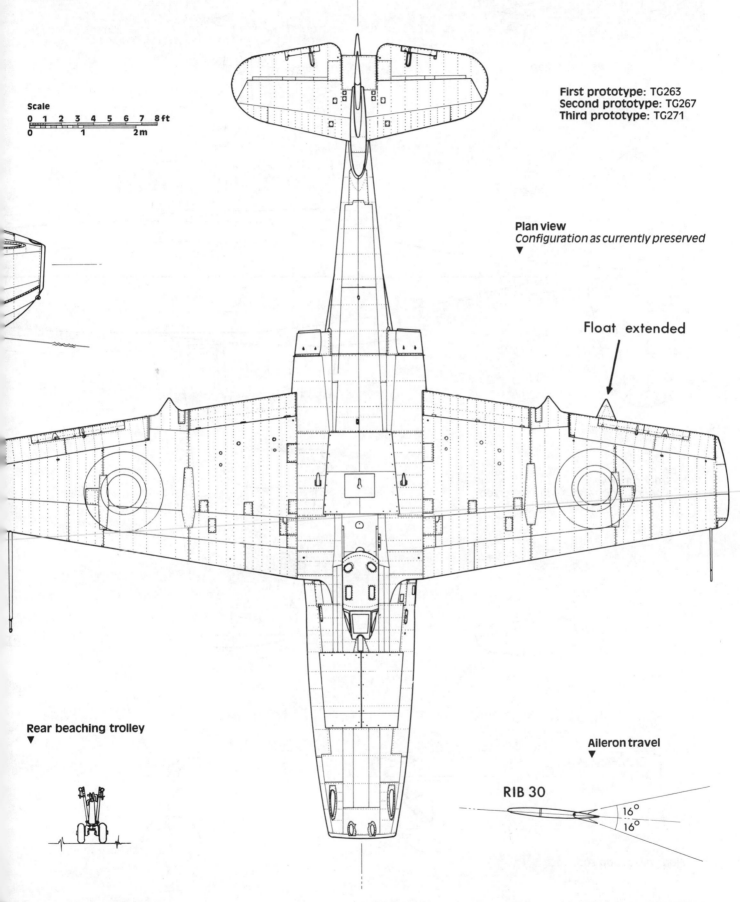

Float extended

Rear beaching trolley
▼

Aileron travel
▼

RIB 30

16°
16°

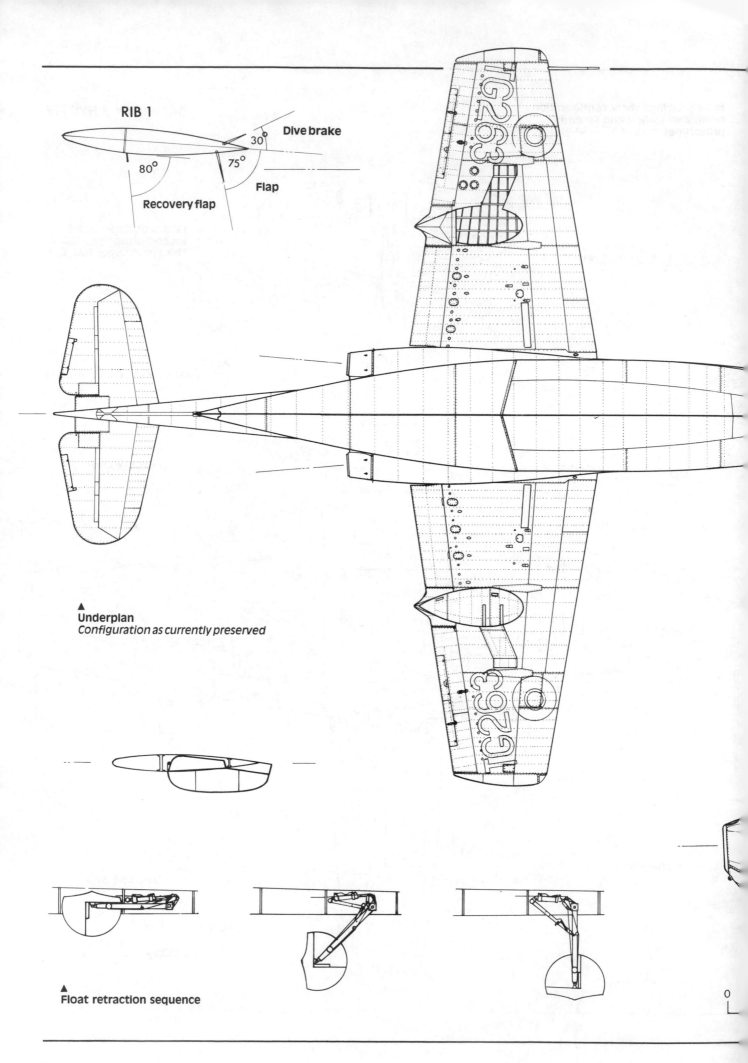

RIB 1

Dive brake

30°

80°

75°

Recovery flap

Flap

▲ **Underplan**
Configuration as currently preserved

▲ **Float retraction sequence**

First of the three SRA/1 jet-powered flying boats. This aircraft survives today, preserved at IWM Duxford. ▶

Scrap port elevation
Intake splitter and extension actuating rod
▼

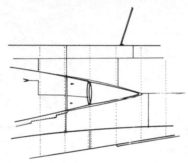

▲
Scrap port elevation
Exhaust fairing, third prototype

Port elevation
Configuration as at first flight
▼

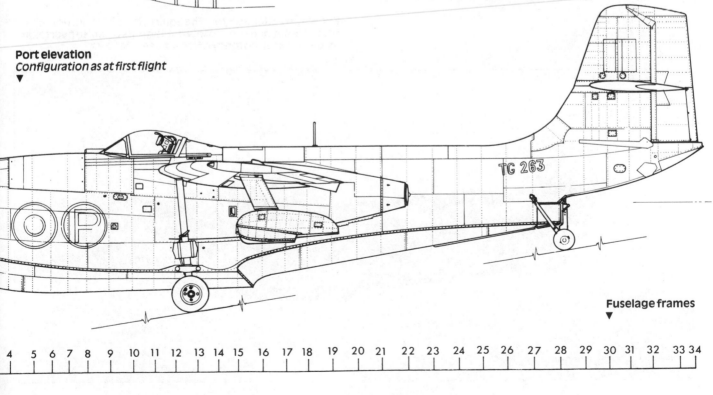

TG 263

Fuselage frames
▼

4 5 6 7 8 9 10 11 12 13 14 15 16 17 18 19 20 21 22 23 24 25 26 27 28 29 30 31 32 33 34

Hull cross-sections

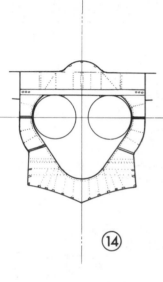

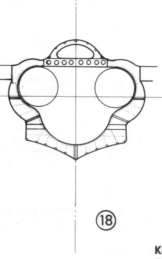

Known affectionately as 'The Squirt', the SRA/1 did not progress beyond the prototype stage, its promise overtaken by the growing potency of land-based fighters.
▼

Mikoyan/Gurevich MiG-15 ('Fagot')

Country of origin: USSR.
Type: Single-seat, land-based fighter.
Dimensions: Wing span 33ft 1½in *10.10m*; length 36ft 4in *11.10m*; height 11ft 2in *3.40m*; wing area 186.7 sq ft *17.25m²*.
Weights: Empty 8331lb *3780kg*; loaded

11,284lb *5120kg*; maximum 14,249lb *6465kg*.
Powerplant: One RD45 turbojet of 5450lb *2471kg* static thrust.
Performance: Maximum speed 670mph *1080kph*; initial climb rate 10,400ft/min *3170m/min*; service ceiling 51,000ft

15,550m; endurance about 2hr.
Armament: One fixed 37mm N cannon and two fixed 23mm NS cannon, plus (optional) up to 2000lb *907kg* of bombs or rockets.
Service: First flight (prototype) 2 July 1947; service entry 1949.

Scale
0 1 2 3 4 5 6 7 8 ft
0 1 2m

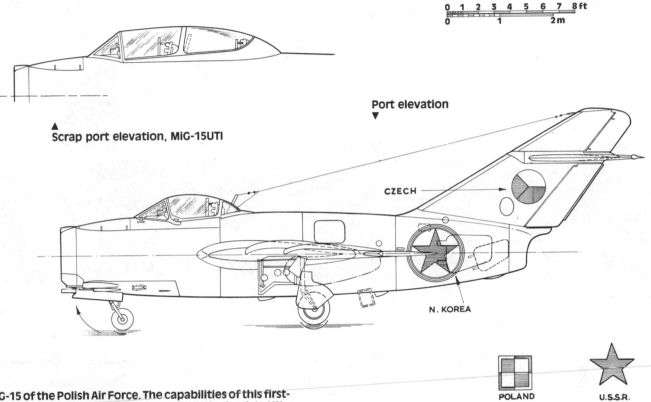

▲
Scrap port elevation, MiG-15UTI

Port elevation
▼

CZECH

N. KOREA

POLAND

U.S.S.R.

MiG-15 of the Polish Air Force. The capabilities of this first-generation Soviet jet fighter came as a rude shock to UN forces during the Korean War.
▼

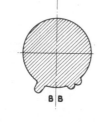

A A

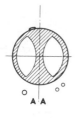

B B

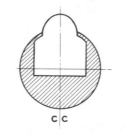

C C

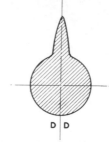

D D

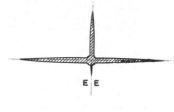

E E

◄ **Fuselage cross-sections**

Wing and tailplane cross-sections
▼

F F

G G

H H

◄ **Captured Egyptian MiG-15 on display in Israel. It is over 40 years since this design first flew, yet many examples are still in service.**

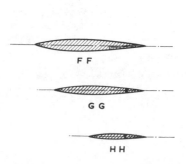

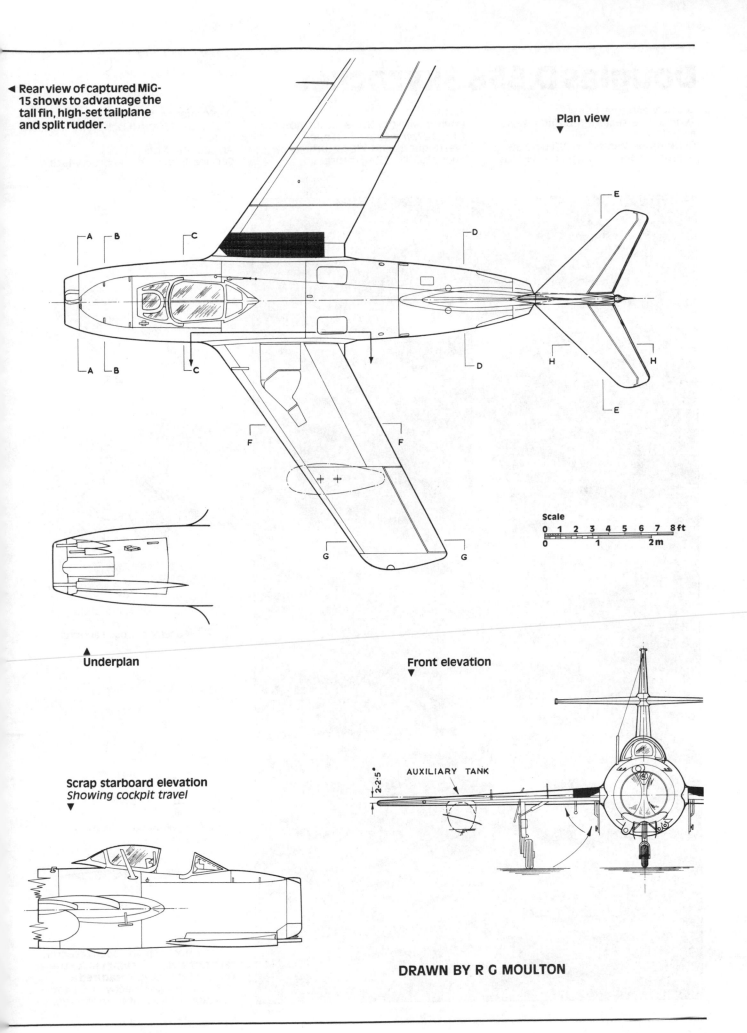

◀ Rear view of captured MiG-15 shows to advantage the tall fin, high-set tailplane and split rudder.

Plan view ▼

Scale

| 0 | 1 | 2 | 3 | 4 | 5 | 6 | 7 | 8 ft |

| 0 | | 1 | | 2 m |

Underplan ▲

Front elevation ▼

AUXILIARY TANK

2·2·5°

Scrap starboard elevation
Showing cockpit travel ▼

DRAWN BY R G MOULTON

Douglas D.558 Skyrocket

Country of origin: USA.
Type: Single-seat, land-based research aircraft.
Dimensions: Wing span 25ft 0in *7.62m*; length 45ft 3in *13.79m*; height 11ft 6in *3.51m*.

Powerplant: One XLR-8 rocket motor of 6000lb *2721kg* thrust, plus one Westinghouse J34-WE-22 turbojet of about 3000lb *1360kg* thrust.

Performance: Maximum speed 1327mph *2136kph* (Mach 2.01) at 65,000ft *19,800m*.
Armament: None.
Service: First flight 4 February 1948.

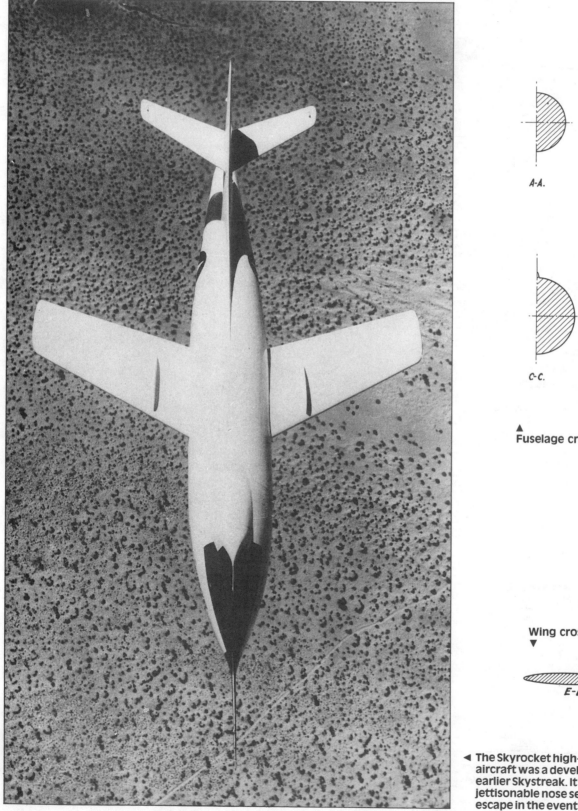

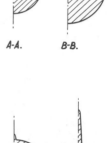

A-A.   B-B.

C-C.   D-D.

▲ **Fuselage cross-sections**

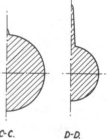

Wing cross-section
▼

E-E

◄ The Skyrocket high-speed research aircraft was a development of the earlier Skystreak. It featured a jettisonable nose section for pilot escape in the event of an emergency.

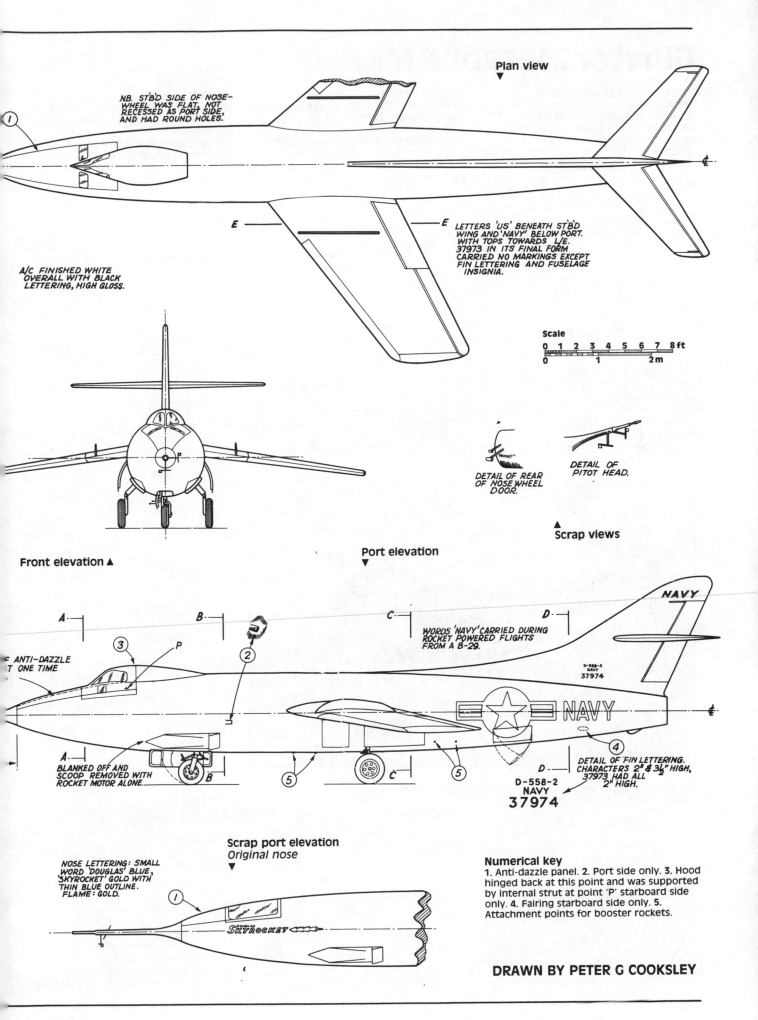

Plan view ▼

NB. ST'B'D SIDE OF NOSE-WHEEL WAS FLAT, NOT RECESSED AS PORT SIDE, AND HAD ROUND HOLES.

LETTERS 'US' BENEATH ST'B'D WING AND 'NAVY' BELOW PORT, WITH TOPS TOWARDS L/E. 37973 IN ITS FINAL FORM CARRIED NO MARKINGS EXCEPT FIN LETTERING AND FUSELAGE INSIGNIA.

A/C FINISHED WHITE OVERALL WITH BLACK LETTERING, HIGH GLOSS.

Scale
0 1 2 3 4 5 6 7 8 ft
0 1 2 m

DETAIL OF REAR OF NOSE WHEEL DOOR.

DETAIL OF PITOT HEAD.

▲ **Scrap views**

Front elevation ▲

Port elevation ▼

WORDS 'NAVY' CARRIED DURING ROCKET POWERED FLIGHTS FROM A B-29.

ANTI-DAZZLE AT ONE TIME

BLANKED OFF AND SCOOP REMOVED WITH ROCKET MOTOR ALONE.

NAVY

D-558-2
NAVY
37974

NAVY

DETAIL OF FIN LETTERING. CHARACTERS 2" & 3½" HIGH, 37973 HAD ALL 2" HIGH.

D-558-2
NAVY
37974

Scrap port elevation
Original nose ▼

NOSE LETTERING: SMALL WORD 'DOUGLAS' BLUE, 'SKYROCKET' GOLD WITH THIN BLUE OUTLINE. FLAME: GOLD.

DOUGLAS SKYROCKET

Numerical key
1. Anti-dazzle panel. 2. Port side only. 3. Hood hinged back at this point and was supported by internal strut at point 'P' starboard side only. 4. Fairing starboard side only. 5. Attachment points for booster rockets.

DRAWN BY PETER G COOKSLEY

Gloster Meteor F Mk 8

Country of origin: Great Britain.
Type: Single-seat, land-based fighter.
Dimensions: Wing span 37ft 2in *11.33m*; length 43ft 6in *13.26m*; height 13ft 10in *4.22m*.
Weights: Empty 10,626lb *4821kg*; loaded (clean) 15,675lb *7112kg*; maximum

17,250lb *7827kg*.
Powerplant: Two Rolls-Royce Derwent 8 turbojets each of 3600lb *1633kg* static thrust.
Performance: Maximum speed 592mph *953kph* at sea level; initial climb rate 7000ft/min *2135m/min*; service ceiling

44,000ft *13,400m*; range 710 miles *1150km*.
Armament: Four fixed 20mm Hispano cannon.
Service: First flight (prototype F Mk 8) 12 October 1948; service entry 10 December 1949.

Port elevation ▼

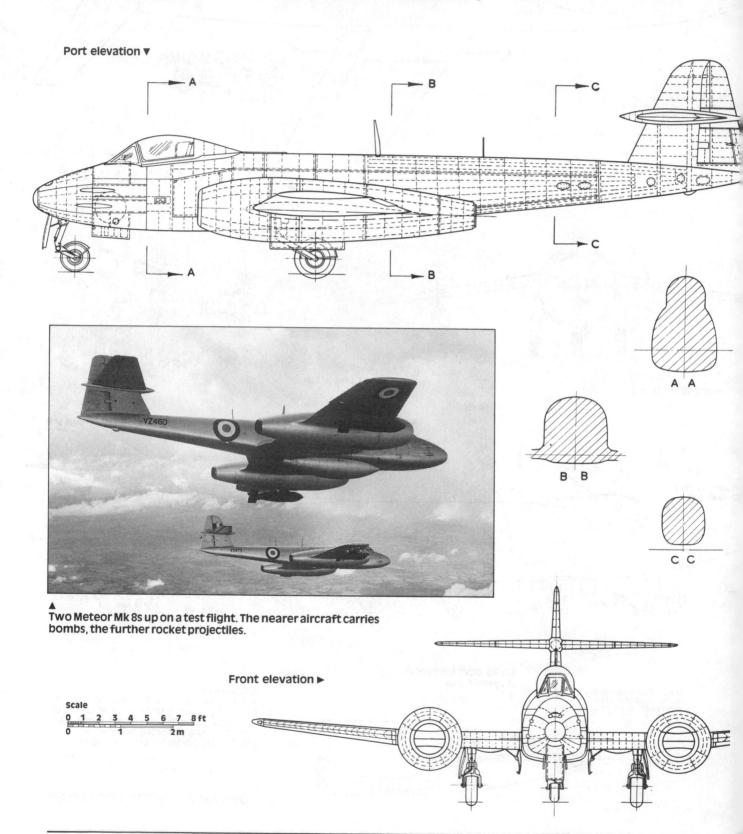

▲
Two Meteor Mk 8s up on a test flight. The nearer aircraft carries bombs, the further rocket projectiles.

Front elevation ►

Scale
0 1 2 3 4 5 6 7 8 ft
0   1   2m

A A

B B

C C

▲
Close-in view of the nose shows the cannon ports and ejector chutes, and the conformal belly tank.

◄ Fuselage cross-sections

Wing cross-section
▼

Plan view ▶

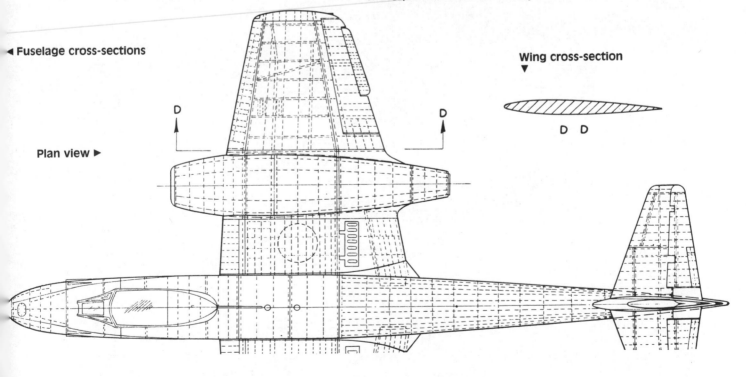

D   D

D   D

De Havilland Vampire T Mk 11

Country of origin: Great Britain.
Type: Two-seat, land-based advanced trainer.
Dimensions: Wing span 38ft 0in *11.58m*; length 34ft 6½in *10.53m*; wing area 261 sq ft *24.25m²*.

Weights: Loaded 11,150lb *5059kg*; maximum 12,920lb *5862kg*.
Powerplant: One De Havilland Goblin 35 turbojet of 3500lb *1588kg* static thrust.
Performance: Maximum speed 550mph *885kph* at 20,000ft *6100m*; initial climb

rate 4500ft/min *1370m/min*; range (clean) 850 miles *1370km*.
Armament: Four fixed 20mm cannon.
Service: First flight (prototype T Mk 11) 15 November 1950.

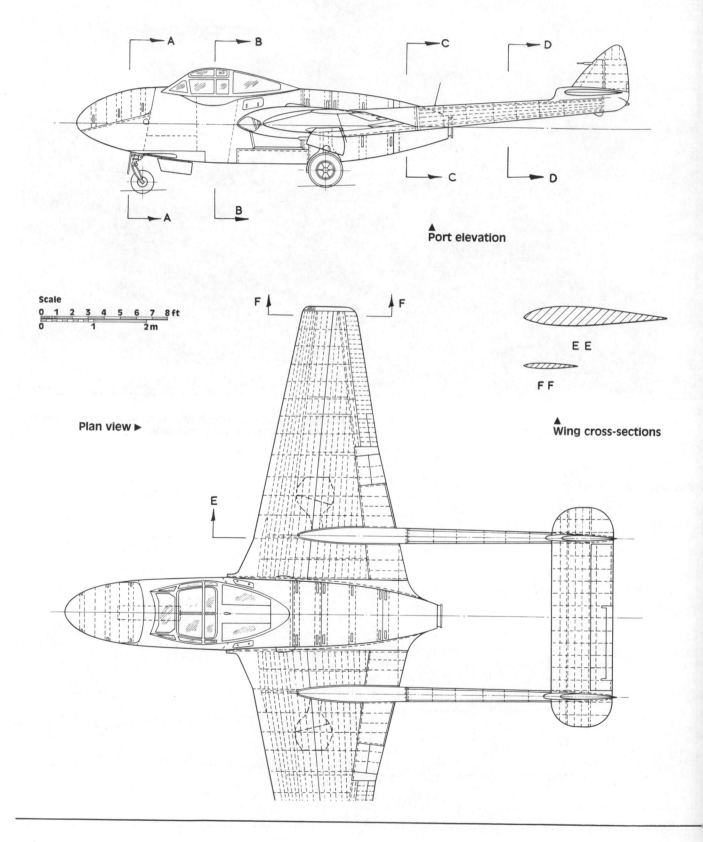

Port elevation

Scale
0 1 2 3 4 5 6 7 8ft
0   1   2m

Plan view ▶

E E

F F

Wing cross-sections

Fuselage and tailboom cross-sections ▶

Production Vampire T.11s, with revised canopies and tailfins and sporting yellow trainer bands.
▼

A A

B B

C C

D D

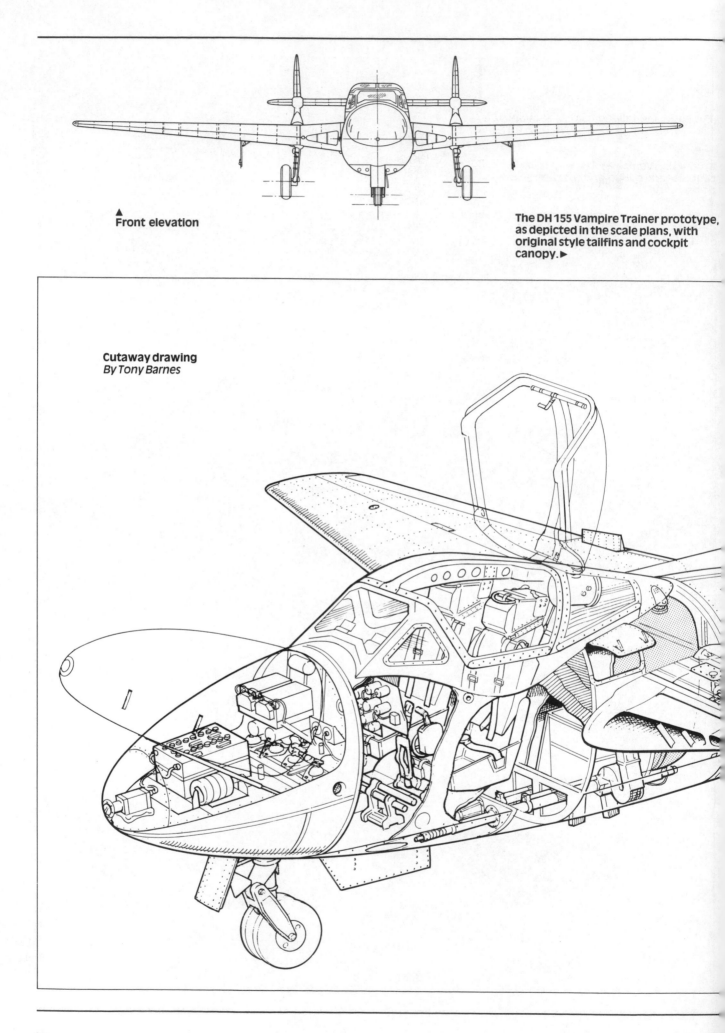

▲
Front elevation

The DH 155 Vampire Trainer prototype, as depicted in the scale plans, with original style tailfins and cockpit canopy. ▶

Cutaway drawing
By Tony Barnes

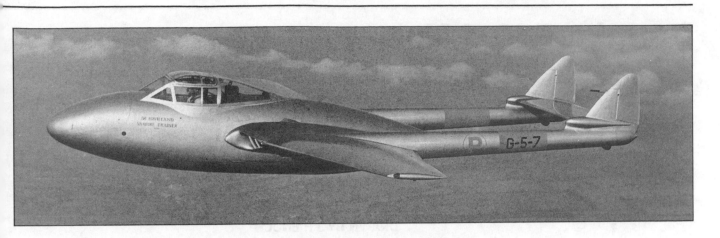

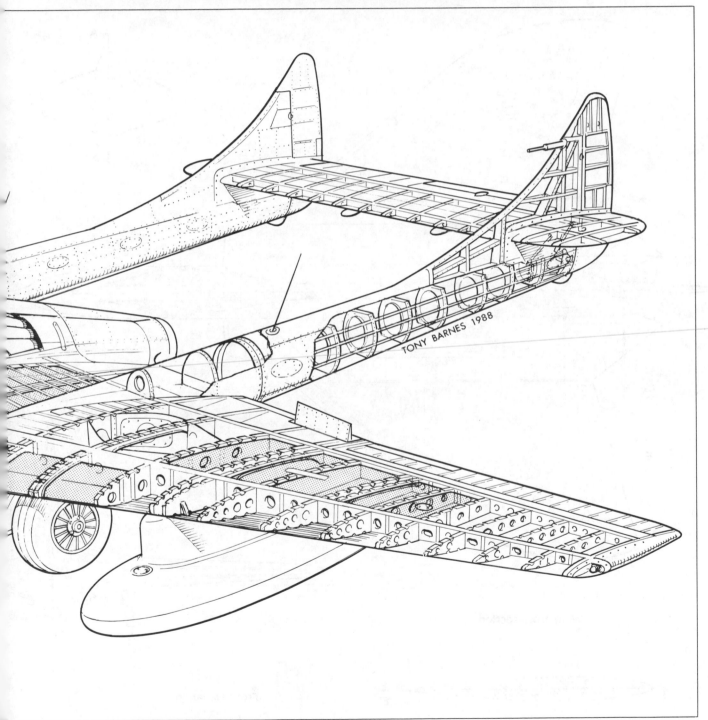

TONY BARNES 1988

Douglas F4D-1 Skyray

Country of origin: USA.
Type: Single-seat, carrier-based, general-purpose fighter and fighter-bomber.
Dimensions: Wing span 33ft 6in *10.21m*; length 45ft 8¼in *13.93m*; height 13ft 0in *3.96m*; wing area 557 sq ft *13.93m²*.

Weights: Loaded about 21,000lb *9524kg*.
Powerplant: One Pratt & Whitney J57-P-8 afterburning turbojet of 14,500lb *6576kg* maximum thrust.
Performance: Maximum speed Mach 1.05 at 36,000ft *10,950m*; initial climb rate 18,000ft/min *5485m/min*; service ceiling

55,000ft *16,765m*; range (external fuel) 950 miles *1530km*.
Armament: Four fixed 20mm cannon, plus up to 4000lb *1814kg* of external ordnance.
Service: First flight (XF4D-1) 23 January 1951, (F4D-1) 5 June 1954.

Plan view
▼

DRAWN BY J R ENOCH

A
A

E   E

E

Wing cross-section
▼

E

▲
Front elevation

28

Scale

0 1 2 3 4 5 6 7 8 ft
0 1 2 m

Port elevation ▼

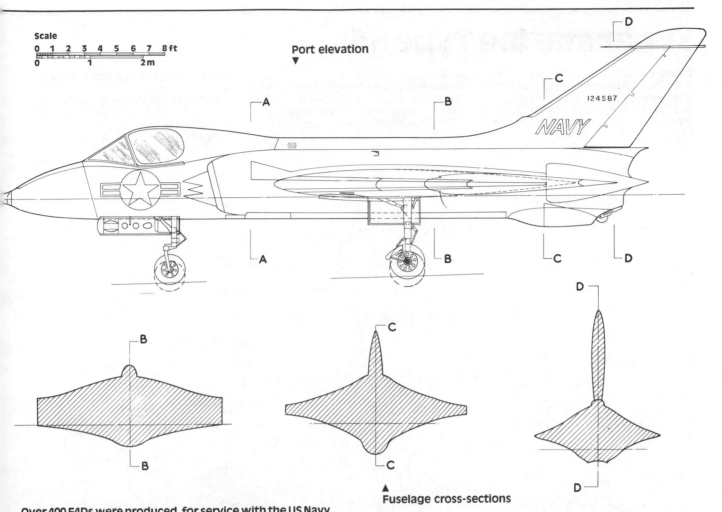

A B C D

124587

NAVY

B B

C C

D D

▲ **Fuselage cross-sections**

Over 400 F4Ds were produced, for service with the US Navy and Marine Corps. The second prototype achieved a world speed record of 752.9mph in October 1953.
▼

Supermarine Type 541

Country of origin: Great Britain.
Type: Prototype single-seat, land-based interceptor fighter.
Dimensions: Wing span 32ft 4in *9.86m*; length 41ft 5½in *12.64m*; height 13ft 6in *4.11m*.
Powerplant: One Rolls-Royce Avon RA7 turbojet of 7000lb *3175kg* thrust.
Performance: Maximum speed about 720mph *1160kph*.
Armament: Two fixed 30mm Aden cannon.
Service: First flight 1 August 1951.

Front elevation ▼

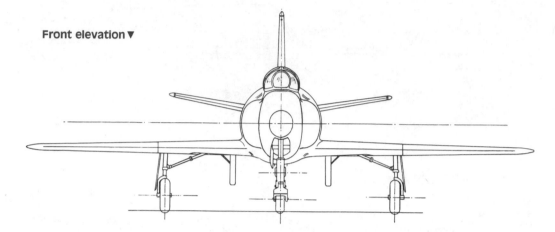

▲ **Fuselage cross-sections**

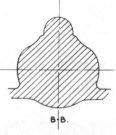

A-A.   B-B.   C-C.

The Type 541 was placed in production as the Swift, but as a fighter the aircraft proved to have poor flying characteristics. Some success was achieved by the aircraft in the reconnaissance role: this is an FR Mk 5 (Type 549) of No 2 Squadron, seen in March 1957.
▼

Scale

0 1 2 3 4 5 6 7 8 ft
0   1   2 m

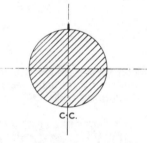

DD.

▲ **Wing cross-section**

DRAWN BY G A CULL

▲
An FR.5, showing the lengthened nose and new canopy of the
fighter-reconnaissance variant. A Swift Mk 4 briefly held the
world speed record for a period in 1953.

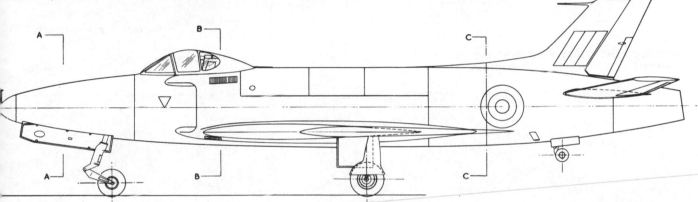

▲
Port elevation

Plan view
▼

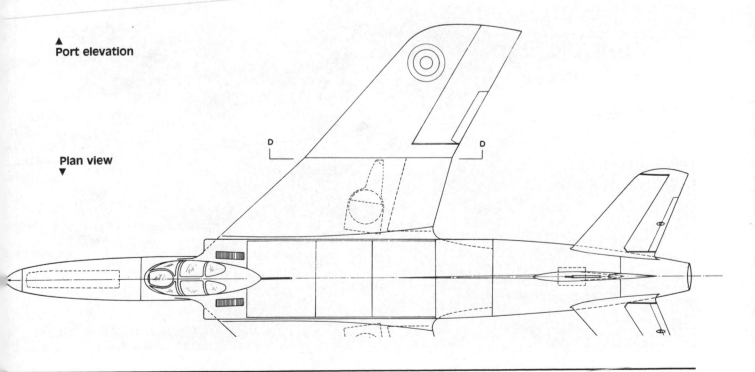

Vickers Valiant B Mk 1

Country of origin: Great Britain.
Type: Long-range, land-based strategic bomber, (B(PR) Mk 1) bomber/photographic-reconnaissance aircraft, (B(PR)K Mk 1) bomber/photographic-reconnaissance aircraft/tanker, (B(K) Mk 1) bomber/tanker.
Dimensions: Wing span 114ft 4in *34.85m*; length 108ft 3in *32.99m*; height 32ft 2in *9.80m²*.

Weights: Empty (B(K) Mk 1) 75,880lb *34,413kg*; maximum overload 175,000lb *79,365kg*.
Powerplant: Four Rolls-Royce Avon RA28 Mk 204 turbojets each of 10,000lb *4535kg* thrust, plus (optional) two De Havilland Super Sprite jettisonable rocket packs.
Performance: Maximum speed 414mph *667kph* at sea level, Mach 0.84 at altitude; initial climb rate 4000ft/min *1220m/min*;

service ceiling about 50,000ft *15,240m*; range (maximum external fuel) 4500 miles *7250km*.
Armament: (B Mk 1) Up to 21,000lb *9525kg* of bombs.
Service: First flight (prototype) 18 May 1951; service entry (B Mk 1) February 1955.

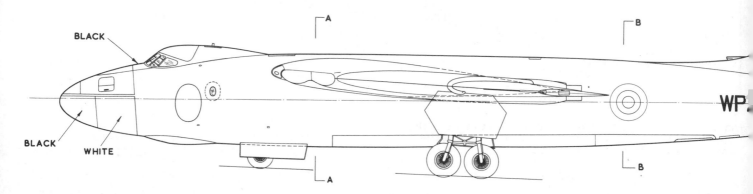

The Valiant was the first of Britain's trio of 'V-bombers', designed for high-altitude nuclear attack.
▼

▲ Port elevation.

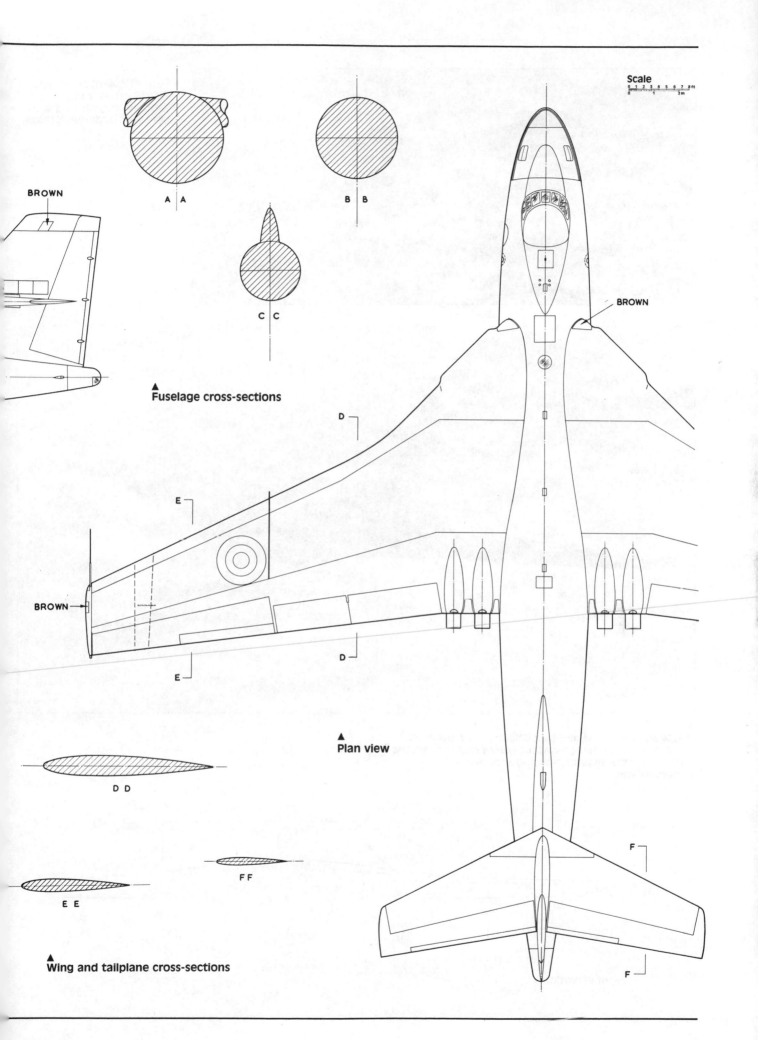

BROWN

Fuselage cross-sections

A A

B B

C C

Scale

Plan view

D

E

BROWN

D

E

D D

E E

F F

BROWN

F

F

Wing and tailplane cross-sections

◄ Second Valiant prototype WB215, powered by Sapphire engines and seen here with underwing tanks.

▲
WJ954 was the single, all-black Valiant B Mk 2: the most obvious external change was the pair of tapered nacelles outboard of the engines, housing a redesigned undercarriage.

Front elevation ▲

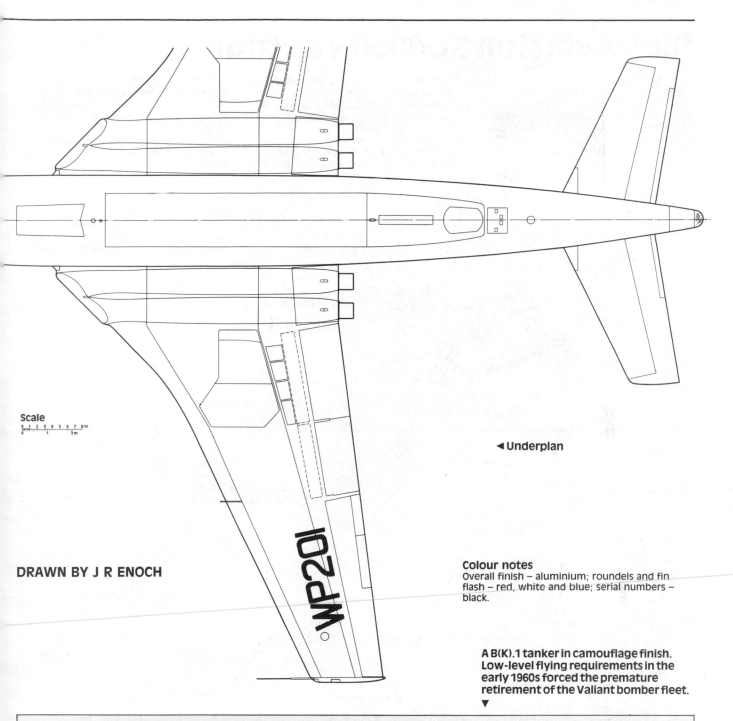

Scale

0 1 2 3 4 5 6 7 8ft
0   1   2m

◄ **Underplan**

DRAWN BY J R ENOCH

WP201

Colour notes
Overall finish – aluminium; roundels and fin flash – red, white and blue; serial numbers – black.

A B(K).1 tanker in camouflage finish. Low-level flying requirements in the early 1960s forced the premature retirement of the Valiant bomber fleet.
▼

Sud-Aviation SO4050 Vautour

Country of origin: France.
Type: Two-seat, land-based light bomber or all-weather fighter, or single-seat, land-based fighter-bomber.
Dimensions: Wing span 49ft 6in *15.09m*; length (exc nose probe) 51ft 1in *15.57m*; height 14ft 2in *4.32m*; wing area 484.5 sq ft *45.0m²*.

Weights: Empty about 22,000lb *10,000kg*; loaded about 44,000lb *20,000kg*.
Powerplant: Two SNECMA Atar 101E-3 axial-flow turbojets each of about 7720lb *3500kg* thrust.
Performance: Maximum speed 680mph *1095kph*; initial climb rate 11,500ft/min *3500m/min*; service ceiling over 49,000ft

15,000m; range 1900 miles *3060km*.
Armament: (Production IIA) Four fixed 30mm DEFA cannon, plus up to about 5300lb *2400kg* of internal and external ordnance.
Service: First flight (prototype 001) 16 October 1952, (production IIA) 30 April 1956.

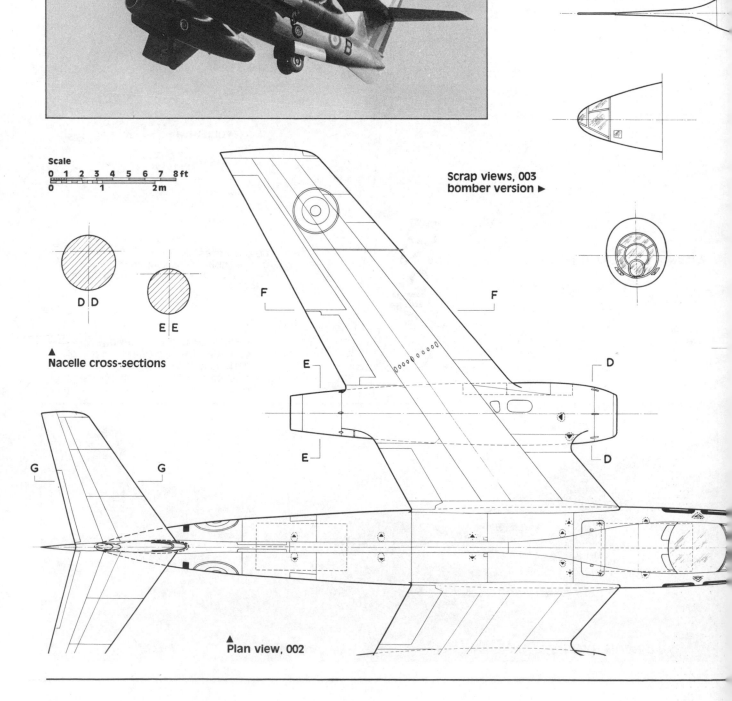

◄ Production Vautour IIA tactical fighter, showing the unusual tandem undercarriage, with outrigger wheels accommodated in the engine nacelles.

Scrap views, 003 bomber version ►

Scale
0 1 2 3 4 5 6 7 8 ft
0 1 2m

▲ Nacelle cross-sections

▲ Plan view, 002

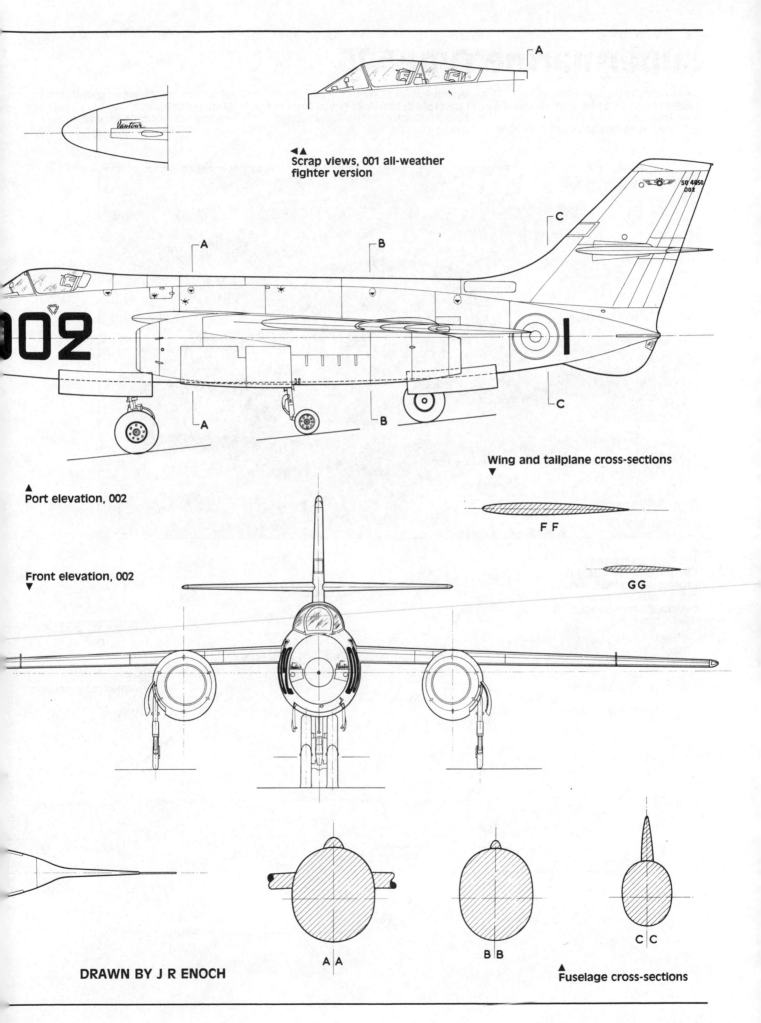

Scrap views, 001 all-weather fighter version

Port elevation, 002

Front elevation, 002

Wing and tailplane cross-sections

F F

G G

Fuselage cross-sections

A A

B B

C C

DRAWN BY J R ENOCH

Supermarine Type 525

Country of origin: Great Britain.
Type: Prototype single-seat, carrier-based fighter.
Dimensions: Wing span 38ft 6in *11.73m*;

length 55ft 0in *16.76m*.
Powerplant: Two Rolls-Royce Avon 114 turbojets each of 7175lb *5254kg* static thrust.

Performance: Maximum speed about 700mph *1125kph*.
Service: First flight 28 April 1954.

▲
The Type 525 started life as the butterfly-tailed third prototype Type 508, and the design was eventually developed into the Scimitar fleet fighter.

Plan view ▶

D   D

D D

▲
Wing cross-section

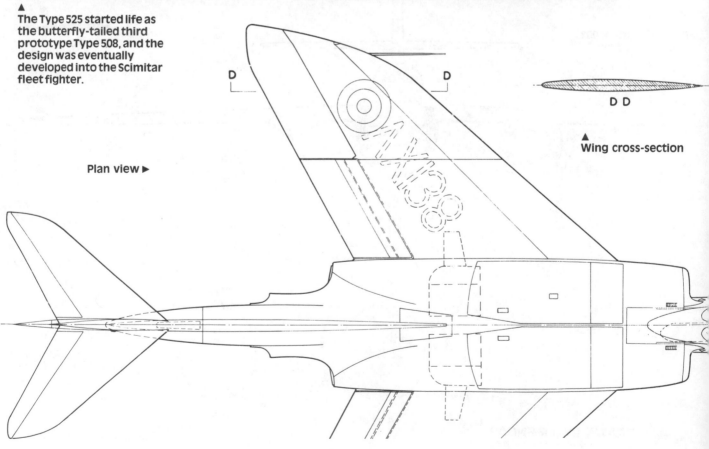

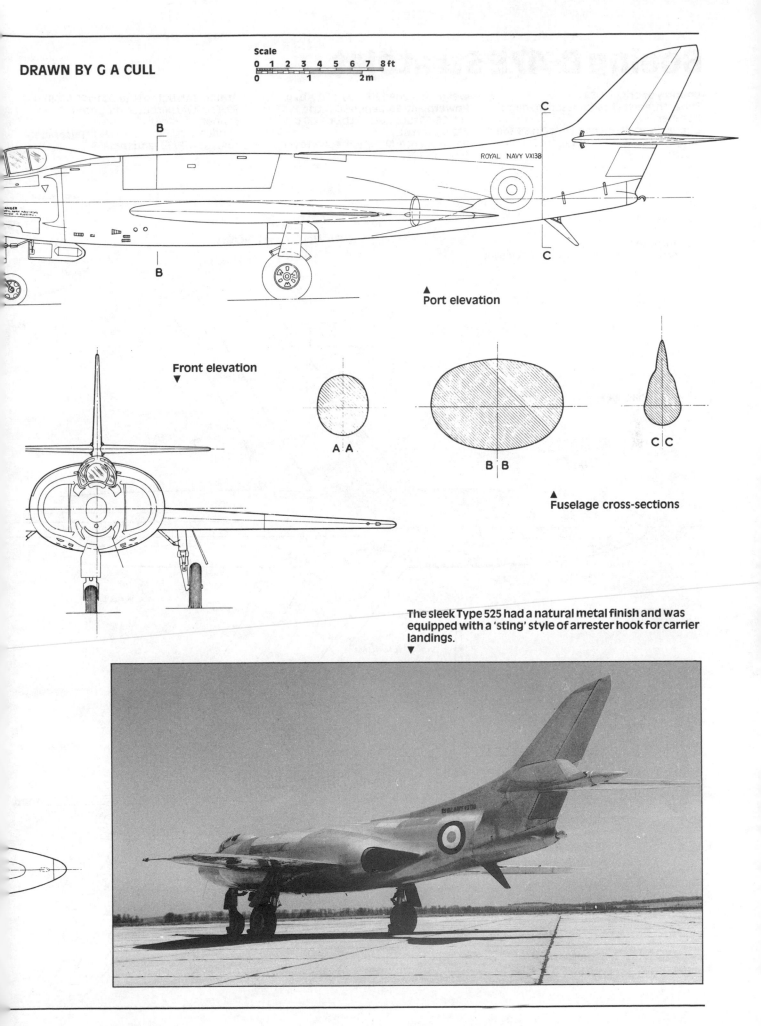

DRAWN BY G A CULL

Scale
0 1 2 3 4 5 6 7 8 ft
0   1   2 m

ROYAL NAVY VX138

▲ Port elevation

Front elevation
▼

A A

B B

C C

▲ Fuselage cross-sections

The sleek Type 525 had a natural metal finish and was equipped with a 'sting' style of arrester hook for carrier landings.
▼

Boeing B-47E Stratojet

Country of origin: USA.
Type: Three-seat, land-based medium bomber.
Dimensions: Wing span 116ft 0in *35.36m*; length 107ft 0in *32.61m*; height 28ft 0in *8.53m*.

Weights: Loaded 200,000lb *90,703kg*.
Powerplant: Six General Electric J47-GE-25 turbojets each of 6000lb *2721kg* thrust.
Performance: Maximum speed over 600mph *966kph*.

Armament: Bomb load up to 20,000lb *9070kg*; two barbette-mounted 20mm cannon.
Service: First flight (XB-47) 17 December 1947, (B-47E) 30 January 1953.

Colour notes
Polished metal finish on all surfaces; standard USAF insignia

DRAWN BY J R ENOCH

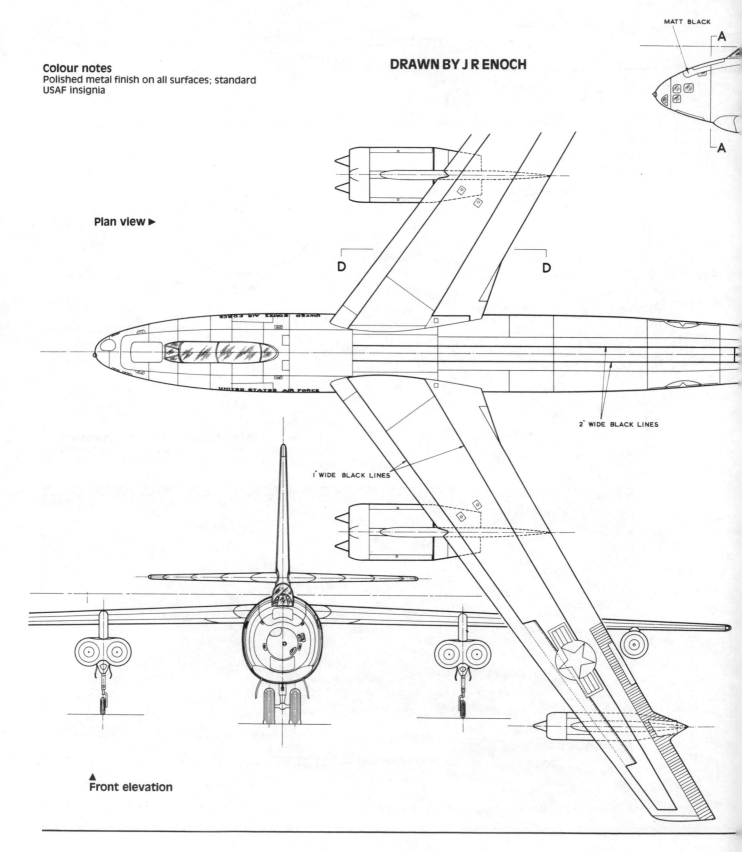

Plan view ►

Front elevation

Port elevation
▼

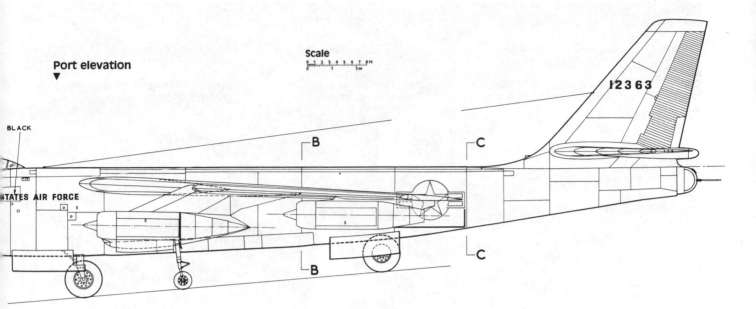

BLACK

STATES AIR FORCE

12363

B B

C C

Scale
0 1 2 3 4 5 6 7 8ft
0 1 2m

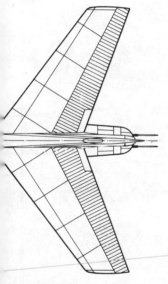

Scrap views, RB-47E
▼

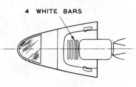

A

A

4 WHITE BARS

XB-47 prototype. The six turbojets were supplemented by eighteen internally mounted Aerojet ATO rockets each of 1000lb thrust – the exhausts for the starboard battery can be seen next to the fuselage insignia.
▼

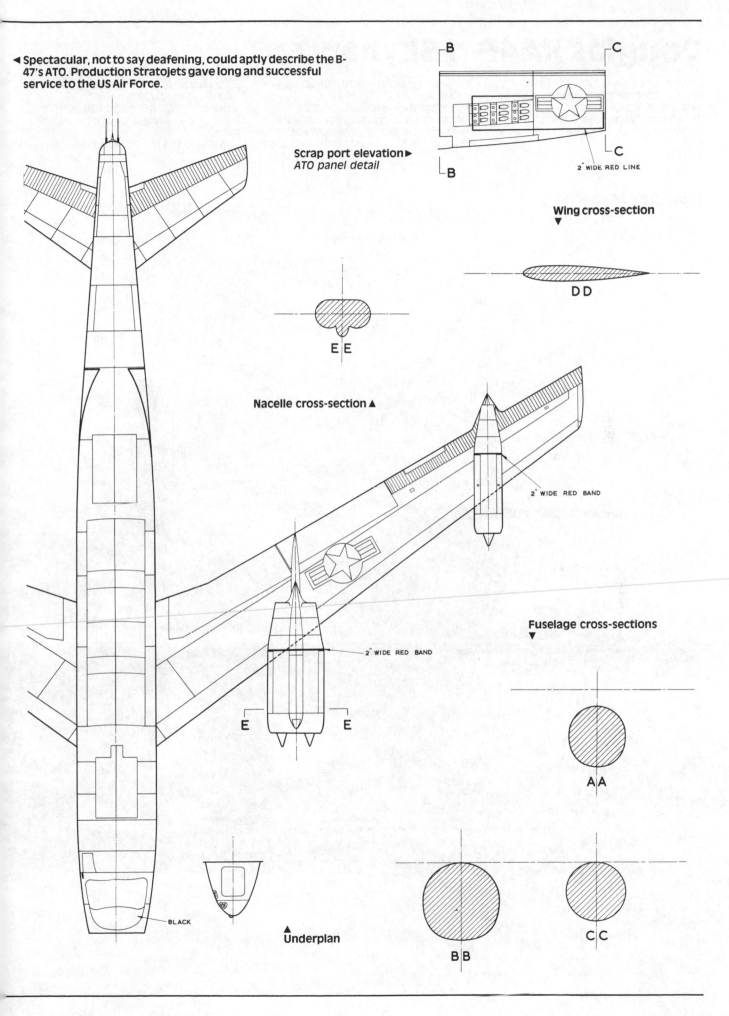

◄ Spectacular, not to say deafening, could aptly describe the B-47's ATO. Production Stratojets gave long and successful service to the US Air Force.

Scrap port elevation►
ATO panel detail

2" WIDE RED LINE

Wing cross-section
▼

D D

E E

Nacelle cross-section ▲

2" WIDE RED BAND

2" WIDE RED BAND

E   E

Fuselage cross-sections
▼

A A

BLACK

▲ Underplan

B B

C C

Douglas XA4D-1 Skyhawk

Country of origin: USA.
Type: Prototype single-seat, carrier-based light attack bomber.
Dimensions: Wing span 27ft 6in *8.38m*; length 39ft 0in *11.89m*; height 15ft 0in *4.57m*.

Weights: Empty about 7500lb *3400kg*; loaded about 15,000lb *6800kg*.
Powerplant: One Wright J65-W-2 turbojet of 7200lb *3265kg* static thrust.
Performance: Maximum speed about 650mph *1050kph*; initial climb rate about

8500ft/min *2590m/min*; service ceiling over 45,000ft *13,700m*.
Armament: Up to 5000lb *2268kg* of external ordnance, plus two fixed 20mm cannon.
Service: First flight 22 June 1954.

DRAWN BY J R ENOCH

Scale

0 1 2 3 4 5 6 7 8 ft

0 1 2m

Port elevation ▼

A   B   C

NAVY   137812

A   B   C

The diminutive Skyhawk was a deliberate – and very successful – attempt to produce a genuinely compact attack aircraft, the design team going to extraordinary lengths to keep the empty weight to an absolute minimum.
▼

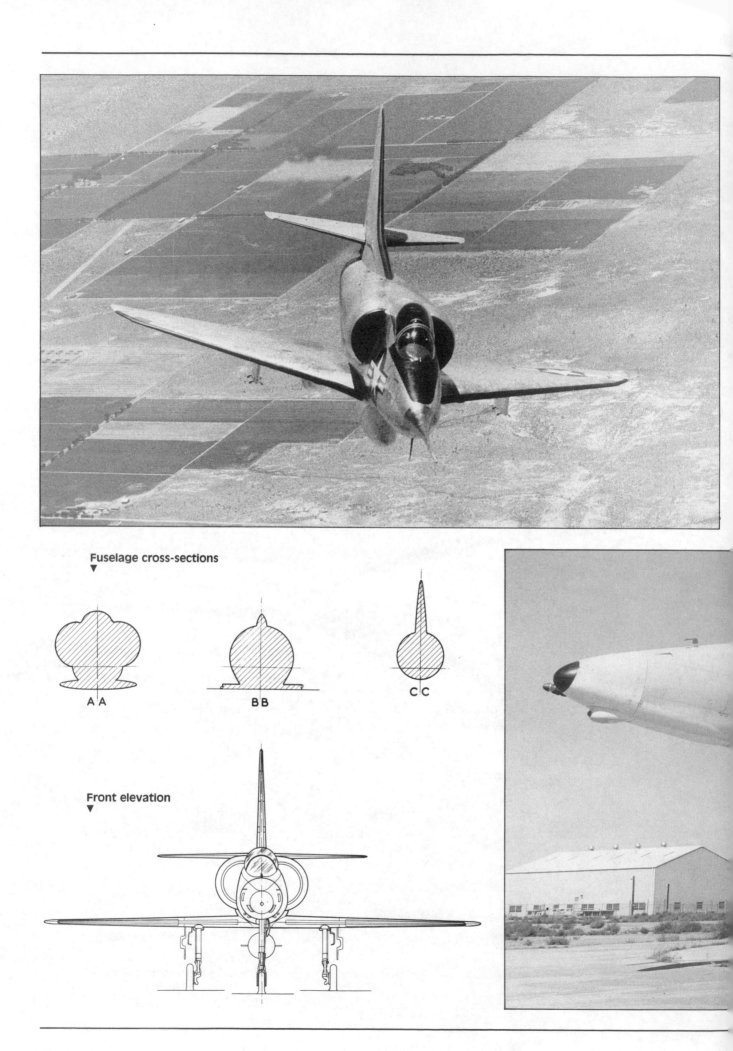

Fuselage cross-sections
▼

A A   B B   C C

Front elevation
▼

D D

E E

▲
Wing and tailplane cross-sections

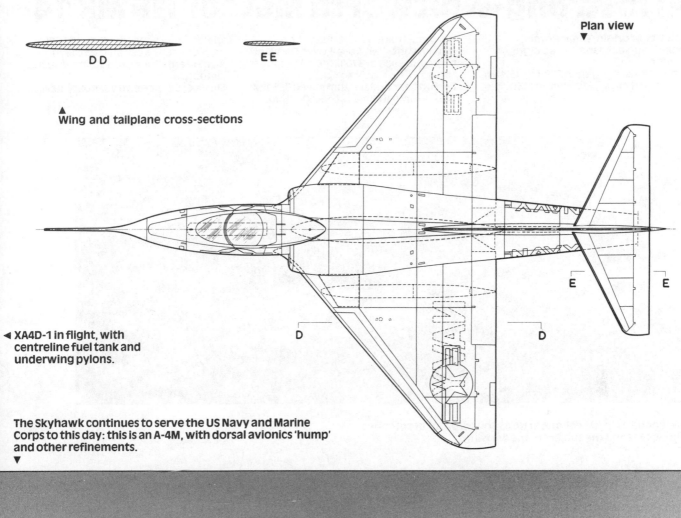

Plan view
▼

E E

D D

◄ **XA4D-1 in flight, with centreline fuel tank and underwing pylons.**

The Skyhawk continues to serve the US Navy and Marine Corps to this day: this is an A-4M, with dorsal avionics 'hump' and other refinements.
▼

Armstrong-Whitworth Meteor NF Mk 14

Country of origin: Great Britain.
Type: Two-seat, land-based night fighter.
Dimensions: Wing span 43ft 0in *13.11m*; length 51ft 4in *15.65m*; height 13ft 10in *4.22m*.

Weights: Loaded 20,444lb *9272kg*.
Powerplant: Two Rolls-Royce Derwent 9 turbojets each of 3700lb *1678kg* static thrust.
Performance: Maximum speed 585mph *941kph*; initial climb rate 6000ft/min

1830m/min; service ceiling 43,000ft *13,100m*; range 950 miles *1530km*.
Armament: Four fixed 20mm Hispano cannon.
Service: Service entry January 1954.

▲
Meteor NF.14 in the colours of No 85 Squadron, photographed about 1954 and the subject of the drawings.

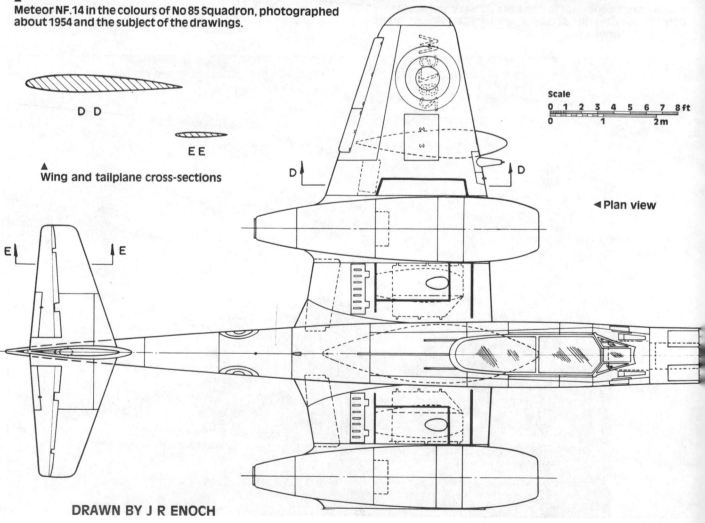

D D

E E

▲
Wing and tailplane cross-sections

Scale

◄ Plan view

DRAWN BY J R ENOCH

Fuselage cross-sections ▶

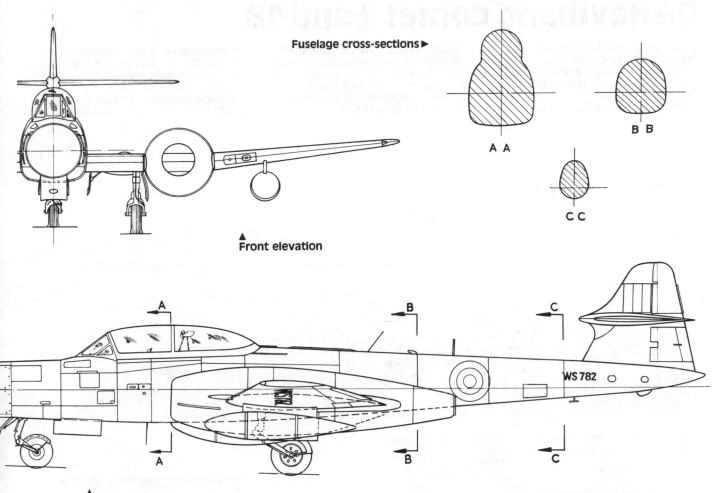

A A

B B

C C

▲ Front elevation

A

B

C

WS 782

A

B

C

▲ Port elevation

No 85 Squadron air crew and their mounts at RAF West Malling.
▼

De Havilland Comet 1 and 4B

Country of origin: Great Britain.
Type: Passenger airliner.
Dimensions: (Comet 4B) Wing span 107ft
10in *32.87m*; length 118ft 0in *35.97m*;
height 29ft 6in *8.99m*.
Weights: (Comet 4B) Basic operational

74,626lb *33,844kg*; maximum loaded
158,000lb *71,655kg*; maximum landing
120,000lb *54,422kg*.
Powerplant: (Comet 4B) Four Rolls-
Royce Avon RA29 Mk 525 turbojets each
of 10,500lb *4762kg* thrust.

Performance: (Comet 4B) Mean cruising
speed 532mph *857kph* at 23,500ft *7165m*;
range at cruising speed with maximum
payload 1840 miles *2960km*.
Service: First flight (Comet 4) 27 April
1958.

Port elevation, Comet 1 ▼

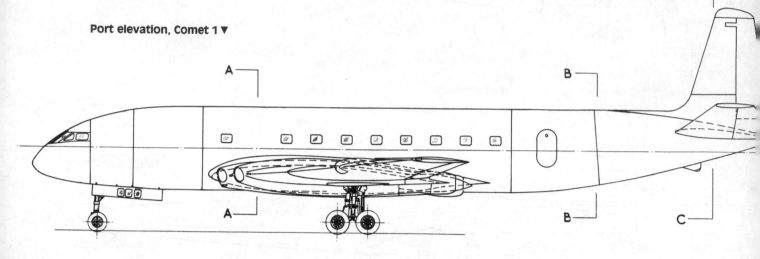

Scale

Fuselage cross-sections, Comet 1
▼

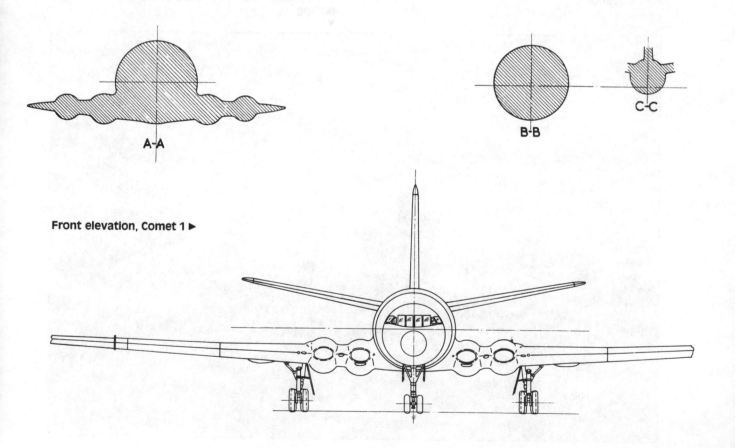

A-A

B-B

C-C

Front elevation, Comet 1 ►

A proud day for British civil aviation: the roll-out of the DH 106
Comet jet airliner at Hatfield on 27 July 1949.

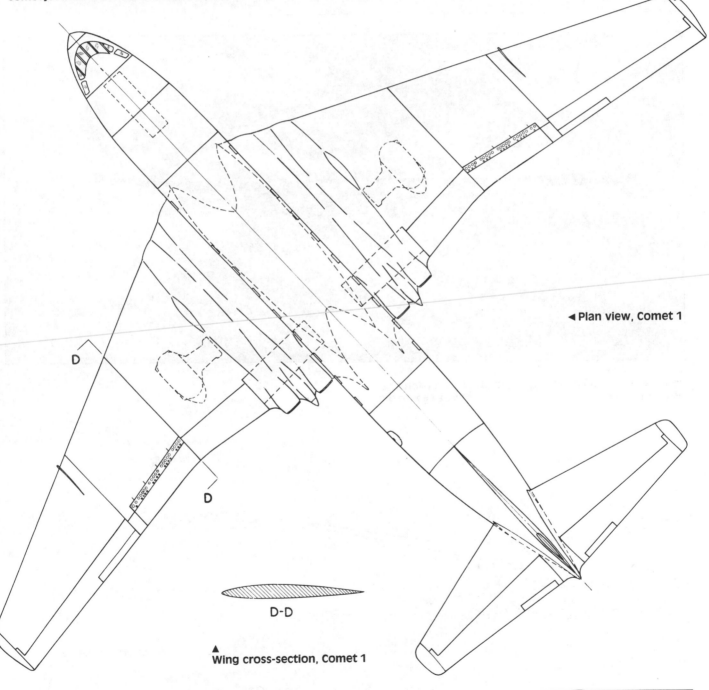

◀ Plan view, Comet 1

D-D

▲ Wing cross-section, Comet 1

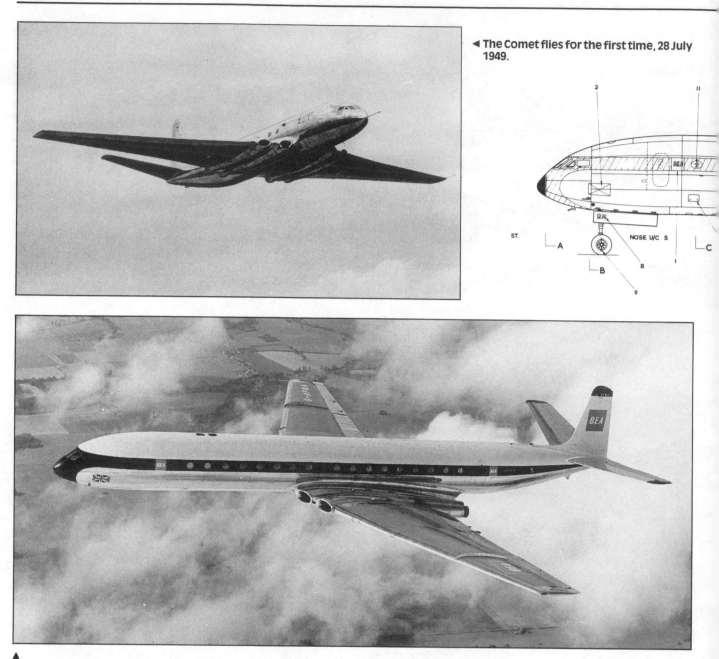

◄ The Comet flies for the first time, 28 July 1949.

▲
Comet 4B in BEA livery. With the arrival of this version, the serious faults of the Comet 1 were shown to be eliminated.

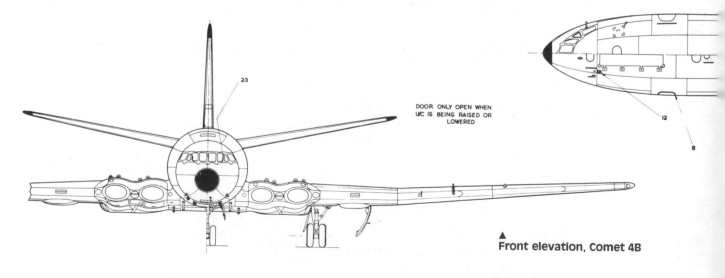

DOOR ONLY OPEN WHEN U/C IS BEING RAISED OR LOWERED

▲
Front elevation, Comet 4B

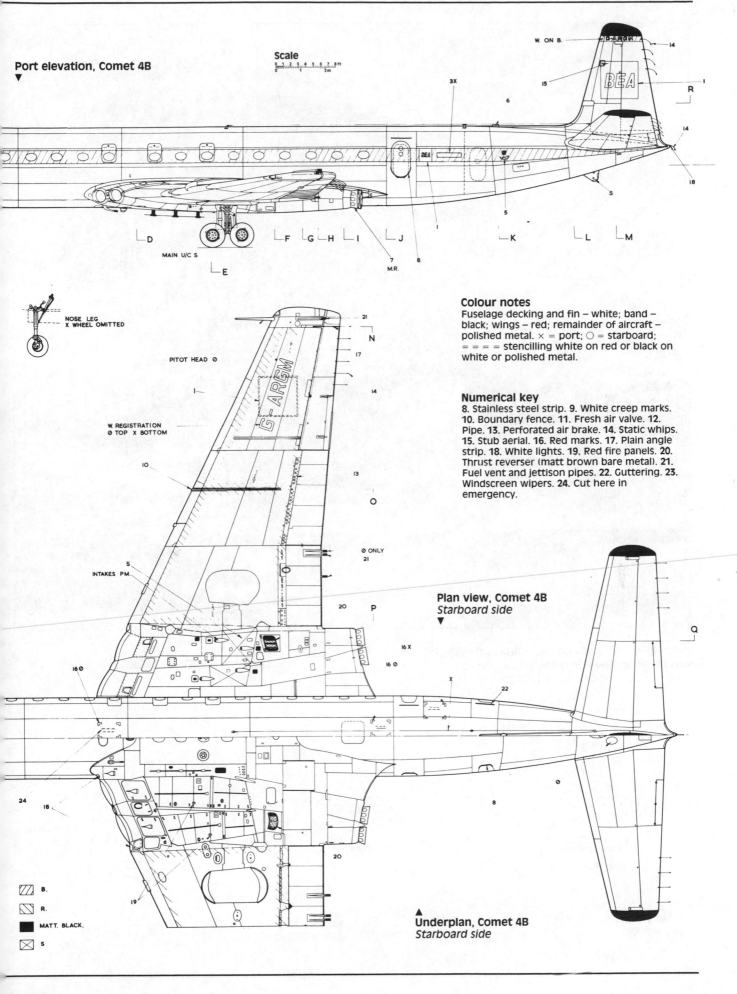

Port elevation, Comet 4B ▼

Scale
0 1 2 3 4 5 6 7 8ft
0   1   2m

MAIN U/C S

D   E   F   G   H   I   J   K   L   M

M.R.

W. ON B.

BEA

R

NOSE LEG
X WHEEL OMITTED

PITOT HEAD Ø

W REGISTRATION
Ø TOP X BOTTOM

INTAKES PM.

S

G-ARGM

Ø ONLY
21

N
17
14
13
O
21
20
P

16 X
16 Ø

X

Plan view, Comet 4B
Starboard side ▼

Q

24
18

B.
R.
MATT. BLACK.
S

Underplan, Comet 4B
Starboard side ▲

Colour notes

Fuselage decking and fin – white; band –
black; wings – red; remainder of aircraft –
polished metal. × = port; ○ = starboard;
= = = = stencilling white on red or black on
white or polished metal.

Numerical key

8. Stainless steel strip. 9. White creep marks.
10. Boundary fence. 11. Fresh air valve. 12.
Pipe. 13. Perforated air brake. 14. Static whips.
15. Stub aerial. 16. Red marks. 17. Plain angle
strip. 18. White lights. 19. Red fire panels. 20.
Thrust reverser (matt brown bare metal). 21.
Fuel vent and jettison pipes. 22. Guttering. 23.
Windscreen wipers. 24. Cut here in
emergency.

▲
**Close-up view of a BEA Comet 4 showing highly polished
natural metal fuselage areas.**

DRAWN BY D H COOKSEY

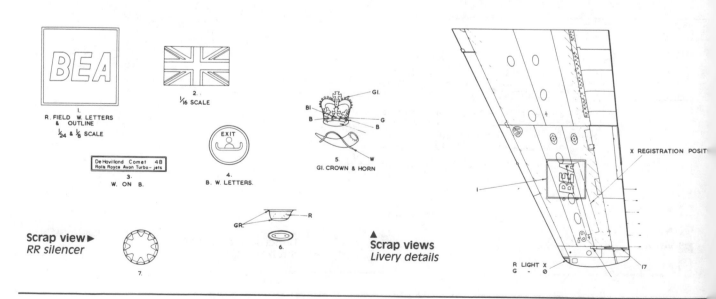

1.
R. FIELD   W. LETTERS
&   OUTLINE
1/24 & 1/8 SCALE

2.
1/16 SCALE

3.
W. ON B.

De Havilland   Comet   4B
Rolls Royce Avon Turbo – jets

EXIT
4.
B. W. LETTERS.

5.
GI. CROWN & HORN

GI.

BI

B

G

B

W

6.
GR.   R

Scrap view ►
RR silencer

7.

▲
Scrap views
Livery details

X REGISTRATION POSIT

I

BEA

R LIGHT X
G – Ø

I7

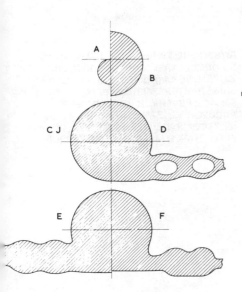

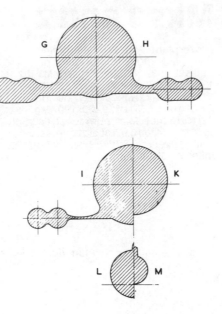

◀ Fuselage cross-sections, Comet 4B

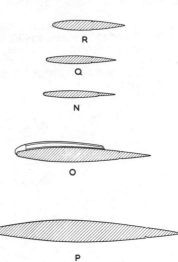

Colour code

B – Black; **Bl** – Blue; **Gl** – Gold; **GR** – Grey; **G** – Green; **R** – Post Box Red; **MR** – Matt brown bare metal; **PM** – Polished metal; **S** – Silver; **W** – White; **ST** – Stainless steel.

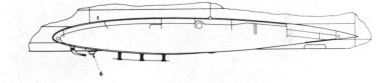

▲ Wing cross-sections, Comet 4B

A Comet 2 (nearest camera) in company with the Comet 3 prototype. The latter was the development aircraft for the Mk 4: note, in particular, the 'stretched' fuselage and the wing tanks.
▼

Avro Vulcan B Mks 1 and 2

Country of origin: Great Britain.
Type: Five-seat, land-based strategic bomber.
Dimensions: Wing span 99ft 0in *30.15m*, (B Mk 2) 111ft 0in *33.83m*; length 97ft 1in *29.61m*, (B Mk 2) 99ft 11in *30.45m*; height 26ft 1in *7.93m*, (B Mk 2) 27ft 2in *8.28m*; wing area 3554 sq ft *330.17m²*, (B Mk 2) 3964 sq ft *368.26m²*.
Weights: Loaded over 200,000lb *90,700kg*.

Powerplant: Four Bristol Siddeley Olympus Mk 101 turbojets each of 11,000lb *4989kg* static thrust or Mk 102 of 12,000lb *5442kg* or Mk 104 of 13,500lb *6122kg*, (B Mk 2) Mk 201 of 17,000lb *7710kg* or Mk 301 of 20,000lb *9070kg*.
Performance: Maximum speed 640mph *1030kph* (Mach 0.97) at altitude; service ceiling over 60,000ft *18,300m*; range 4500 miles *7250km*.

Armament: Twenty-one 1000lb *454kg* bombs or other ordnance up to about 20,000lb *9070kg*, or (B Mk 2) one Avro Blue Steel nuclear missile.
Service: First flight (prototype) 30 August 1952, (B Mk 1) 4 February 1955, (B Mk 2 prototype) 31 August 1957; service entry (B Mk 1) May 1957, (B Mk 2) 1 July 1960.

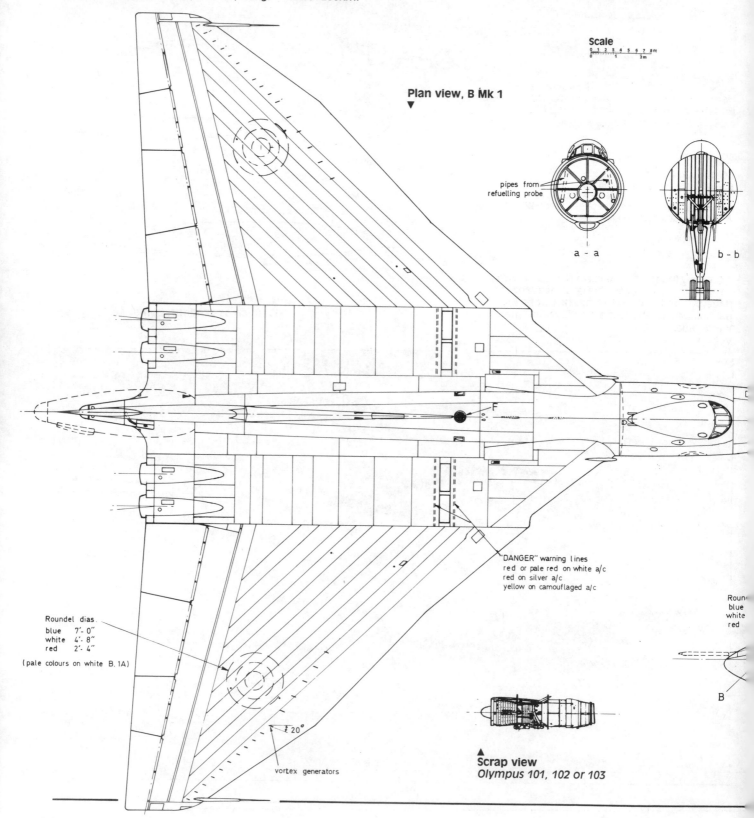

Scale

Plan view, B Mk 1

pipes from refuelling probe

a - a

b - b

'DANGER' warning lines
red or pale red on white a/c
red on silver a/c
yellow on camouflaged a/c

Roundel
blue
white
red

Roundel dias.
blue   7'- 0"
white   4'- 8"
red   2'- 4"

(pale colours on white B. 1A)

20°

vortex generators

B

▲ Scrap view
Olympus 101, 102 or 103

▲
Head-on view of the Vulcan emphasises the aircraft's massive wing-root intakes. Note guard dog and handler – typical of 'V-bomber' bases during the 1950s and 1960s.

Fuselage cross-sections, B Mk 1
▼

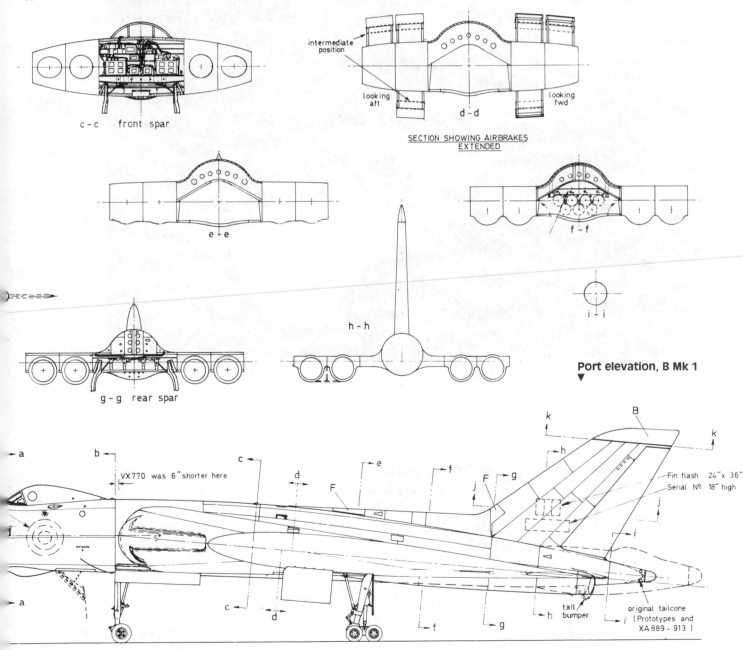

c – c   front spar

intermediate position

looking aft

looking fwd

d – d

SECTION SHOWING AIRBRAKES EXTENDED

e – e

f – f

h – h

i – i

g – g   rear spar

Port elevation, B Mk 1
▼

VX770 was 6″ shorter here

Fin flash 24″ x 36″
Serial № 18″ high

tail bumper

original tailcone
(Prototypes and XA 889 - 913)

57

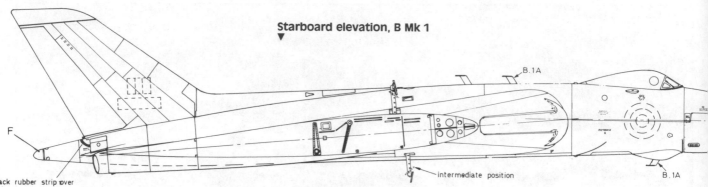

Starboard elevation, B Mk 1
▼

B.1A

intermediate position

B.1A

F

Black rubber strip over
brake parachute strop

**Line up of B.2s in anti-flash white finish and with pale insignia
and serials.**
▼

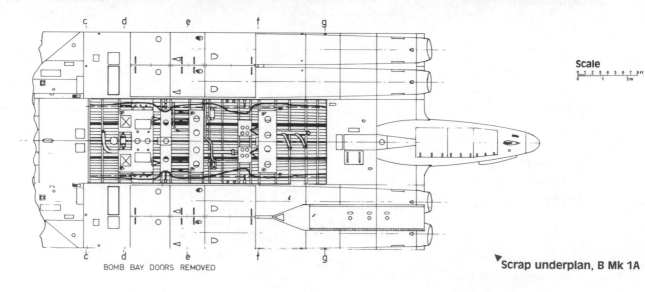

XJ782

c   d   e   f   g

c   d   e   f   g

BOMB BAY DOORS REMOVED

Scale
0 1 2 3 4 5 6 7 8ft
0   1   2m

▼**Scrap underplan, B Mk 1A**

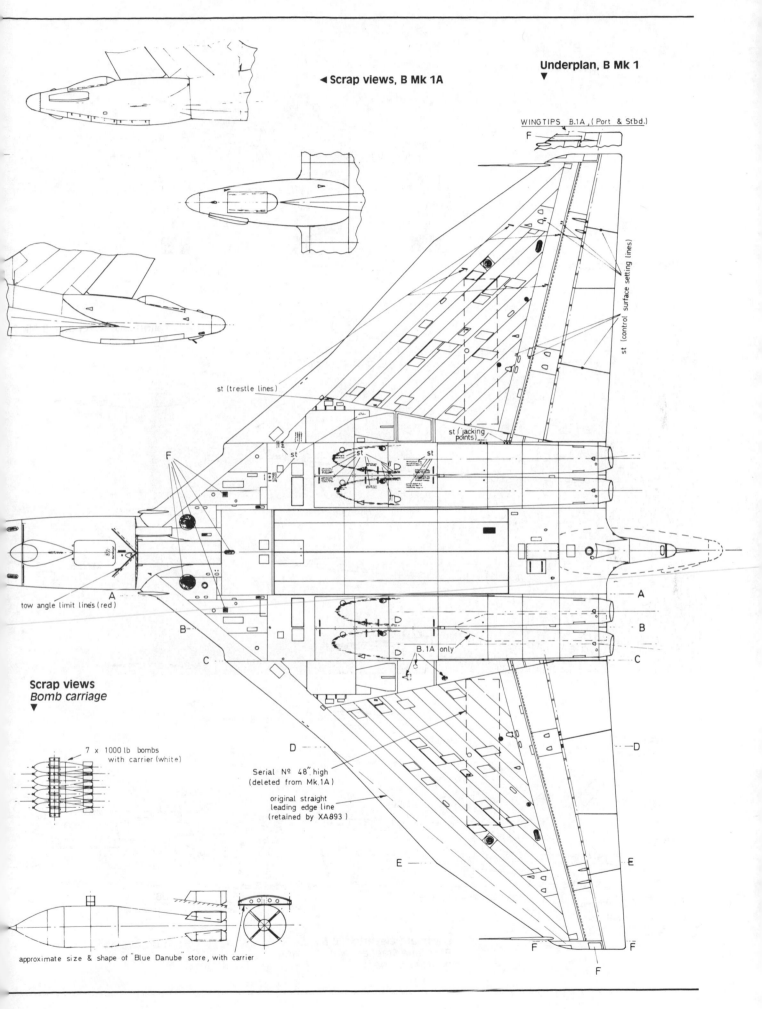

◄ **Scrap views, B Mk 1A**

Underplan, B Mk 1
▼

WINGTIPS B.1A, (Port & Stbd.)

F

st (control surface setting lines)

st (trestle lines)

st (jacking points)

st

st

st

F

A

tow angle limit lines (red)

B

B.1A only

C

Scrap views
Bomb carriage
▼

7 x 1000 lb bombs
with carrier (white)

D

Serial Nº 48″ high
(deleted from Mk.1A)

original straight
leading edge line
(retained by XA893)

E

approximate size & shape of "Blue Danube" store, with carrier

F

A

B

C

D

E

F

F

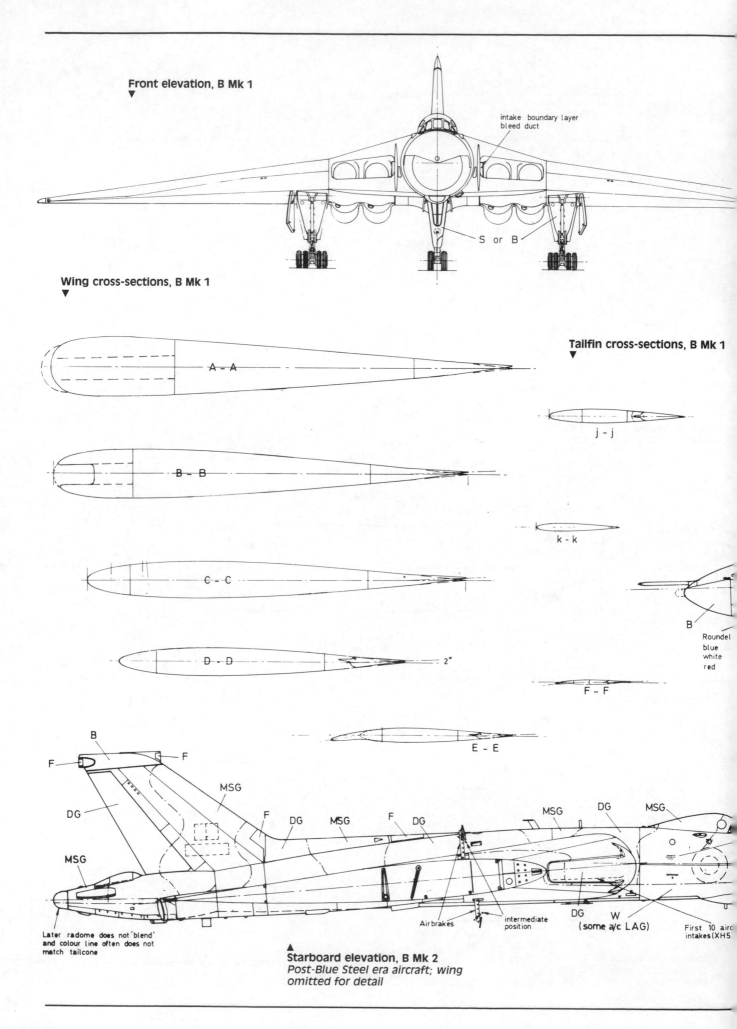

Front elevation, B Mk 1
▼

intake boundary layer
bleed duct

S or B

Wing cross-sections, B Mk 1
▼

A - A

B - B

C - C

D - D   2°

Tailfin cross-sections, B Mk 1
▼

j - j

k - k

B

Roundel
blue
white
red

F - F

E - E

B

F   F

MSG

DG

F   DG   MSG   F   DG

MSG   DG   MSG

MSG

Airbrakes   intermediate
position

DG
(some a/c LAG)

First 10 airc
intakes (XH5

Later radome does not 'blend'
and colour line often does not
match tailcone

▲
Starboard elevation, B Mk 2
*Post-Blue Steel era aircraft; wing
omitted for detail*

Colour code, B Mk 1

W – Anti-radiation white; **B** – Semi-matt black;
S – Silver; **F** – Fibreglass; **LAG** – Light Aircraft
Grey.

Colour notes, B Mk 1

Prototypes VX770 and 777 – white overall;
production aircraft XA889–901 – silver initially;
XA896, 898–901 – white later; XA902–XH532 –
white. Some B.1As (eg XH500) were
camouflaged. Stencilling ('st' on drawings) –
red on silver and white B.1s, pale red on white
B.1As (with pale roundel colours), yellow on
camouflaged aircraft.

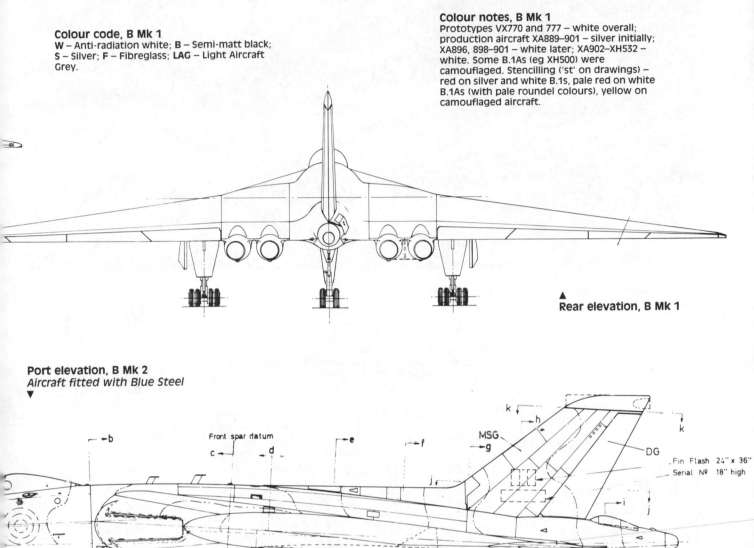

▲ **Rear elevation, B Mk 1**

Port elevation, B Mk 2
Aircraft fitted with Blue Steel
▼

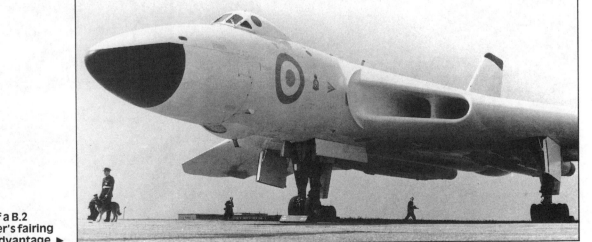

**Low-angle view of a B.2
shows bomb-aimer's fairing
beneath nose to advantage.** ▶

B.2 with dummy Skybolts beneath the wings. These nuclear missiles never entered production.

Scrap underplan, B Mk 2
Normal bomb doors and additional ECM plate between port nacelles
▼

▲
Scrap view
Olympus 301

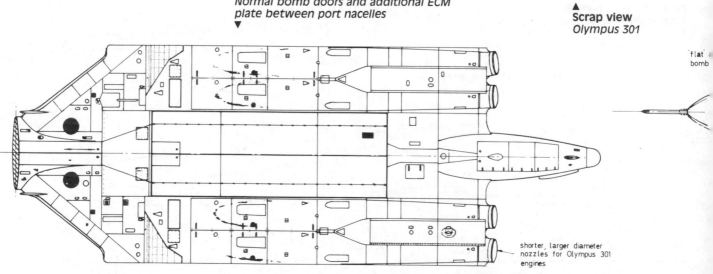

'flat'
bomb

shorter, larger diameter nozzles for Olympus 301 engines

XH539

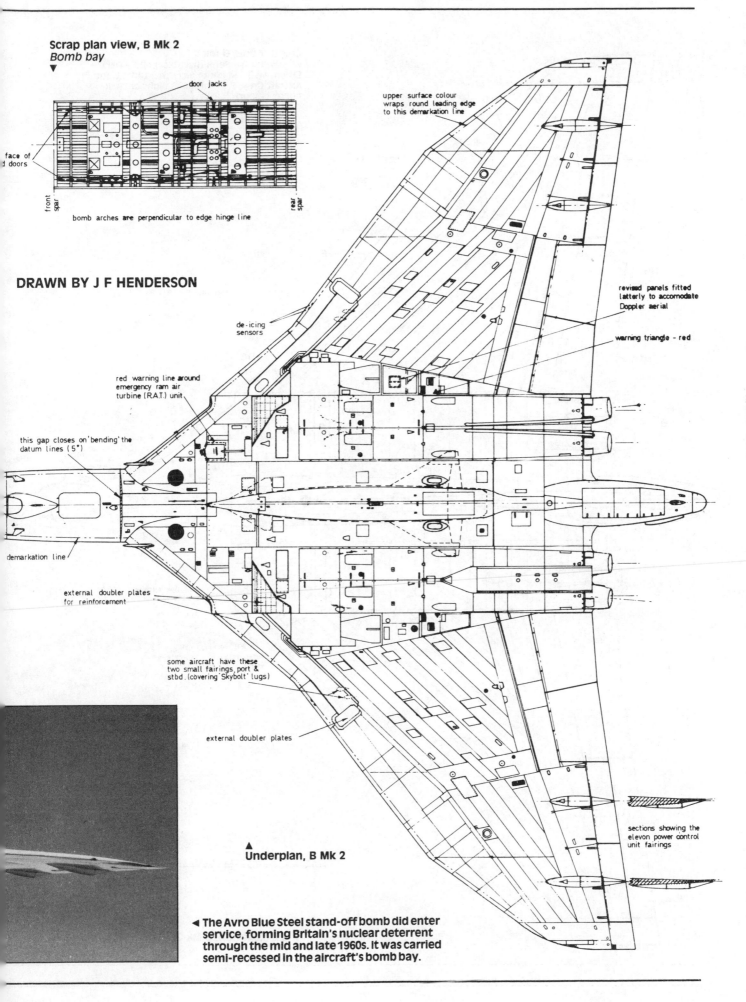

Scrap plan view, B Mk 2
Bomb bay
▼

door jacks

face of
d doors

front spar

rear spar

bomb arches are perpendicular to edge hinge line

DRAWN BY J F HENDERSON

de-icing
sensors

upper surface colour
wraps round leading edge
to this demarkation line

revised panels fitted
latterly to accomodate
Doppler aerial

warning triangle - red

red warning line around
emergency ram air
turbine (R.A.T.) unit

this gap closes on 'bending' the
datum lines (5°)

demarkation line

external doubler plates
for reinforcement

some aircraft have these
two small fairings, port &
stbd. (covering 'Skybolt' lugs)

external doubler plates

sections showing the
elevon power control
unit fairings

▲ **Underplan, B Mk 2**

◄ The Avro Blue Steel stand-off bomb did enter
service, forming Britain's nuclear deterrent
through the mid and late 1960s. It was carried
semi-recessed in the aircraft's bomb bay.

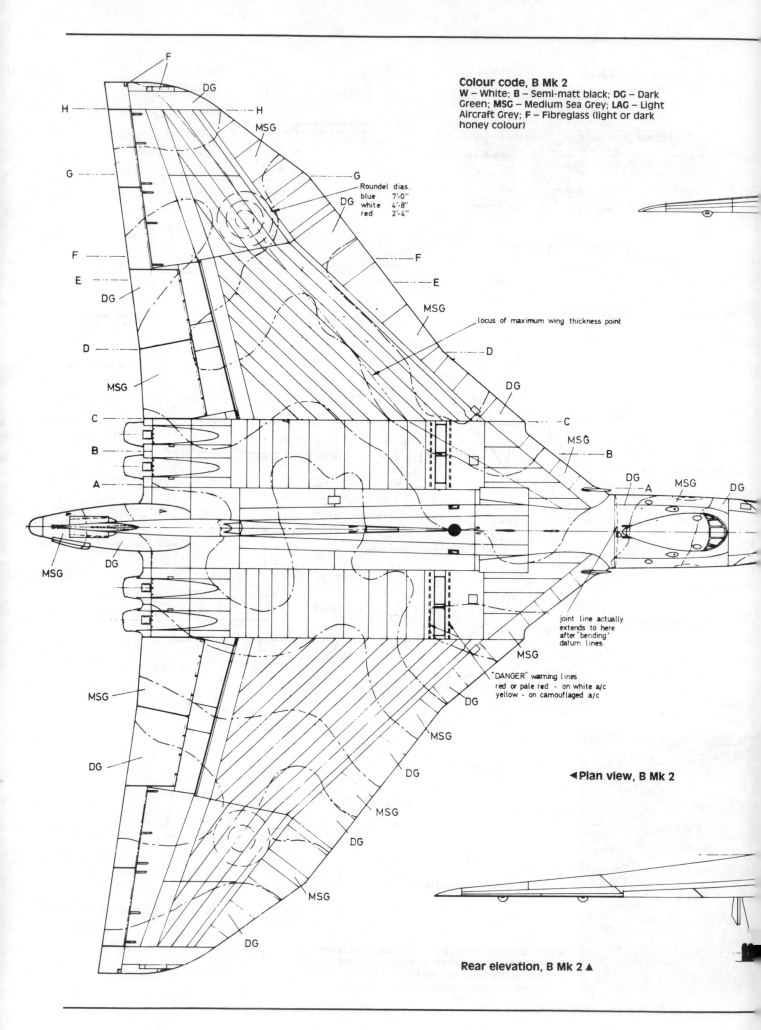

F

DG

H — H

MSG

G — G

Roundel dias.
blue 7'-0"
white 4'-8"
red 2'-4"

DG

F — F

E — E

DG

MSG

locus of maximum wing thickness point

D — D

DG

MSG

C — C

MSG

B — B

DG MSG DG

A — A

MSG

DG

MSG

joint line actually
extends to here
after 'bending'
datum lines

MSG

"DANGER" warning lines
red or pale red - on white a/c
yellow - on camouflaged a/c

DG

MSG

MSG

DG

◄ **Plan view, B Mk 2**

MSG

DG

MSG

Colour code, B Mk 2
W – White; **B** – Semi-matt black; **DG** – Dark
Green; **MSG** – Medium Sea Grey; **LAG** – Light
Aircraft Grey; **F** – Fibreglass (light or dark
honey colour)

Rear elevation, B Mk 2 ▲

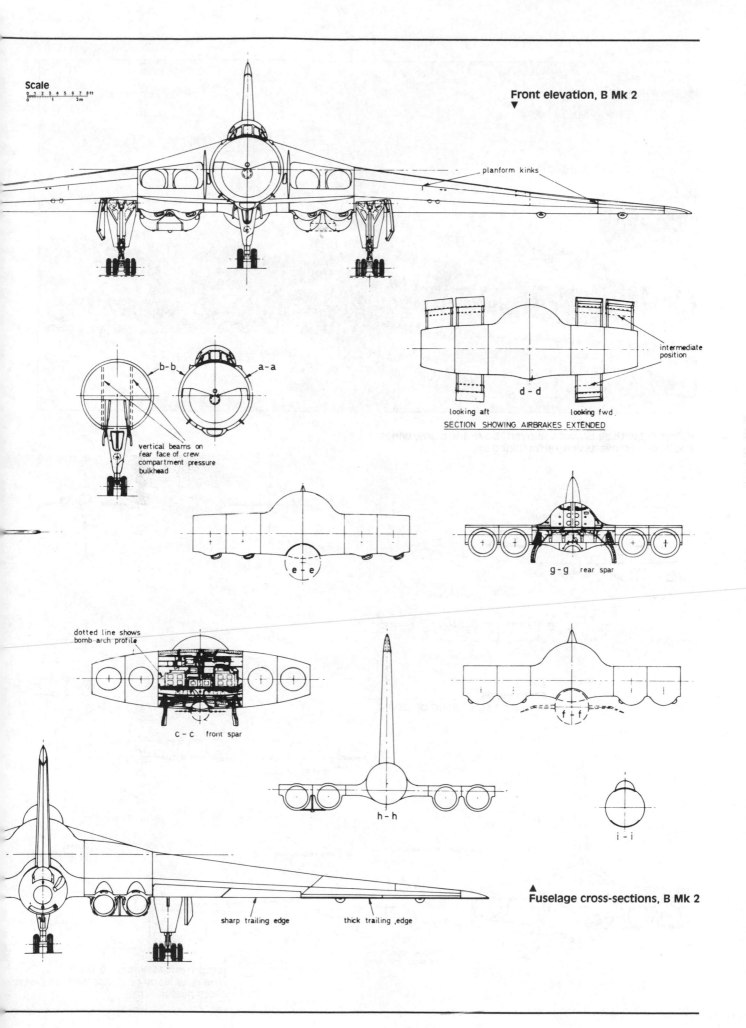

Scale

Front elevation, B Mk 2 ▼

planform kinks

b-b   a-a

vertical beams on
rear face of crew
compartment pressure
bulkhead

intermediate
position

looking aft   looking fwd
SECTION SHOWING AIRBRAKES EXTENDED

d - d

e - e

g - g   rear spar

dotted line shows
bomb arch profile

C - C   front spar

f - f

h - h

i - i

▲ **Fuselage cross-sections, B Mk 2**

sharp trailing edge   thick trailing edge

▲
**Vulcan B.2 with air brakes deployed above and below wings.
The Blue Steel has its ventral fin folded up.**

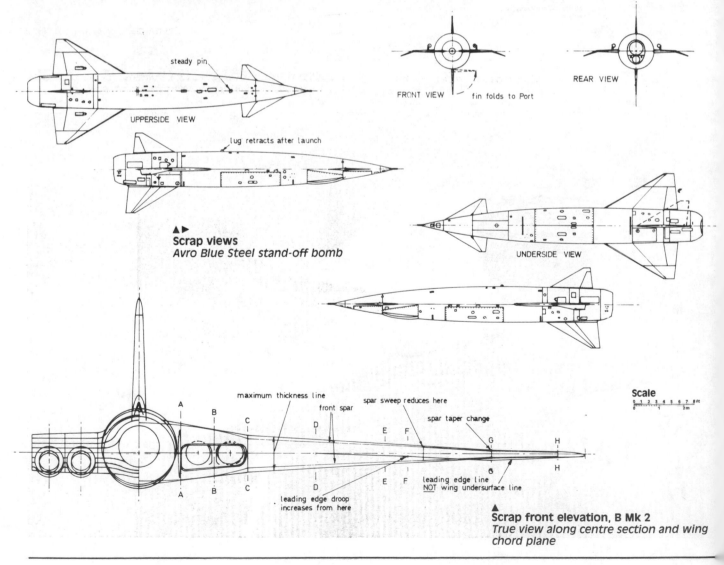

steady pin

UPPERSIDE VIEW

FRONT VIEW   fin folds to Port

REAR VIEW

lug retracts after launch

▲▶
Scrap views
Avro Blue Steel stand-off bomb

UNDERSIDE VIEW

maximum thickness line

front spar

spar sweep reduces here

spar taper change

Scale

leading edge droop
increases from here

leading edge line
NOT wing undersurface line

▲
Scrap front elevation, B Mk 2
*True view along centre section and wing
chord plane*

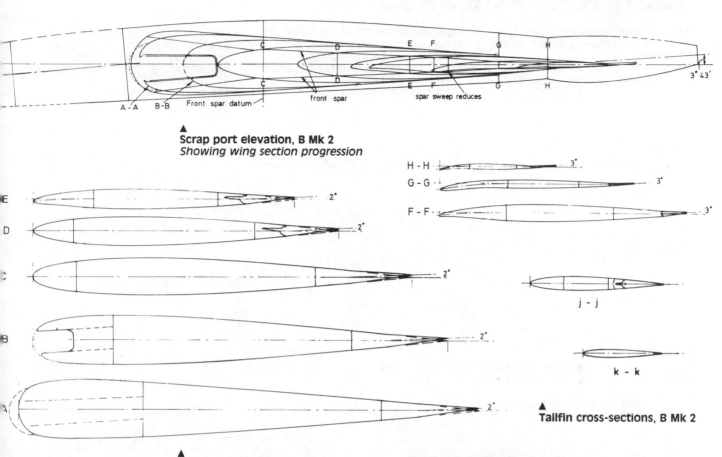

3° 43'

A-A   B-B   Front spar datum   front spar   spar sweep reduces

▲
Scrap port elevation, B Mk 2
Showing wing section progression

E · · · · · · · 2°

D · · · · · · · 2°

C · · · · · · · 2°

B · · · · · · · 2°

A · · · · · · · 2°

H - H · · · · · 3°

G - G · · · · · 3°

F - F · · · · · 3°

j – j

k – k

▲
Tailfin cross-sections, B Mk 2

▲
Wing cross-sections, B Mk 2

For the low-level strike role, Vulcans received a coat of camouflage, with wing roundels to port only.
▼

Saunders-Roe SR53

Country of origin: Great Britain.
Type: Experimental single-seat, land-based interceptor.
Dimensions: Wing span 25ft 1¼in *7.65m*, length 45ft 10in *13.72m*; height 10ft 10in *3.29m*.

Powerplant: One De Havilland Spectre rocket motor of 8000lb *3628kg* static thrust plus one Armstrong Siddeley Viper turbojet of 1750lb *794kg* static thrust.
Performance: Maximum speed

(designed) Mach 2.2; initial climb rate 52,800ft/min *16,100m/min*; service ceiling over 60,000ft *18,300m*.
Armament: (Designed) Two De Havilland Firestreak AAMs.
Service: First flight 16 May 1957.

Front elevation ▶

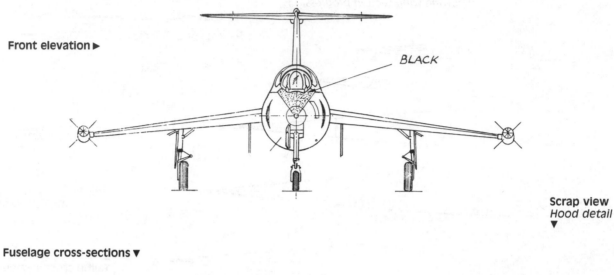

BLACK

Scrap view
Hood detail
▼

Fuselage cross-sections ▼

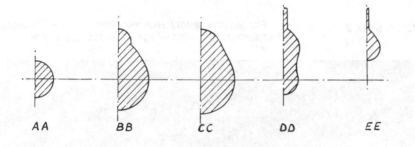

A A   B B   C C   D D   E E

Scale

0 1 2 3 4 5 6 7 8 ft
0   1   2m

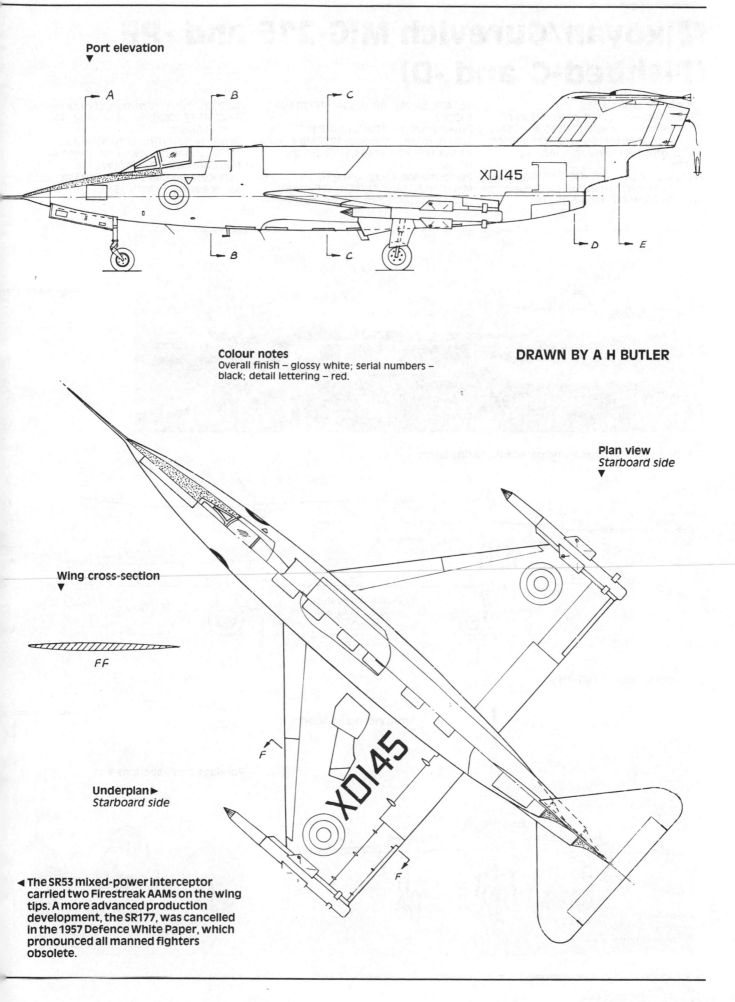

Port elevation

A   B   C

XD145

B   C   D   E

Colour notes
Overall finish – glossy white; serial numbers –
black; detail lettering – red.

DRAWN BY A H BUTLER

Plan view
Starboard side

Wing cross-section

FF

Underplan►
Starboard side

XD145

F

F

◄ The SR53 mixed-power interceptor
carried two Firestreak AAMs on the wing
tips. A more advanced production
development, the SR177, was cancelled
in the 1957 Defence White Paper, which
pronounced all manned fighters
obsolete.

Mikoyan/Gurevich MiG-21F and -PF (Fishbed-C and -D)

Country of origin: USSR.
Type: Single-seat, land-based fighter.
Dimensions: Wing span 23ft 5½in *7.25m*; length (overall) 51ft 8½in *15.76m*; height 13ft 5½in *4.10m*; wing area 247.6 sq ft *23.0m²*.
Weights: Empty (F) 12,440lb *5645kg*; take-off (F, full internal fuel plus centreline tank) 16,700lb *7577kg*, (PF, normal)

18,740lb *8502kg*; maximum (PF) 20,500lb *9300kg*.
Powerplant: One Tumanskii R11F afterburning turbojet of 12,675lb *5750kg* thrust, (PF) R11F2 of 13,115lb *5950kg* thrust.
Performance: Maximum speed (F, clean) Mach 2 at 36,100ft *11,000m*, (PF, clean) Mach 2.02 at 36,100ft; initial climb rate (F)

30,000ft/min *9145m/min*; service ceiling 57,400ft *17,500m*; range (F, clean) 750 miles *1200km*.
Armament: (F) One or two fixed 30mm NR30 cannon plus two underwing AAMs, (PF) underwing AAMs only.
Service: First flight (prototype) late 1955; service entry (F) early 1958.

▲
Fishbed-C with JATO gear and parachute fairing on fin.

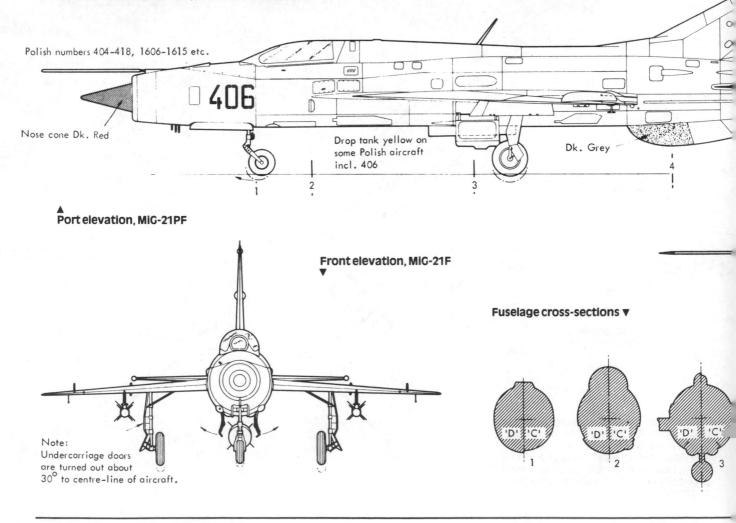

Polish numbers 404–418, 1606–1615 etc.

406

Nose cone Dk. Red

Drop tank yellow on some Polish aircraft incl. 406

Dk. Grey

1 2 3 4

▲
Port elevation, MiG-21PF

Front elevation, MiG-21F
▼

Fuselage cross-sections ▼

Note:
Undercarriage doors are turned out about 30° to centre-line of aircraft.

'D' 'C' 'D' 'C' 'D' 'C'
1 2 3

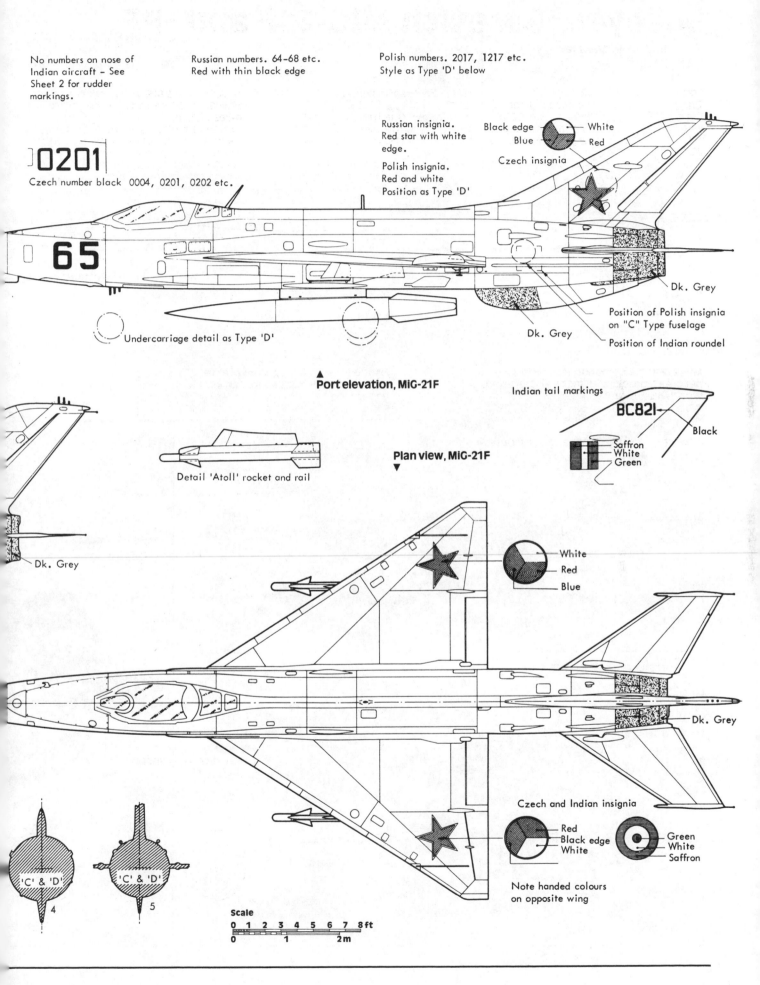

No numbers on nose of
Indian aircraft – See
Sheet 2 for rudder
markings.

Russian numbers. 64–68 etc.
Red with thin black edge

Polish numbers. 2017, 1217 etc.
Style as Type 'D' below

Russian insignia.
Red star with white
edge.

Polish insignia.
Red and white
Position as Type 'D'

Black edge — White
Blue — Red

Czech insignia

0201

Czech number black 0004, 0201, 0202 etc.

65

Dk. Grey

Position of Polish insignia
on "C" Type fuselage

Position of Indian roundel

Dk. Grey

Undercarriage detail as Type 'D'

Port elevation, MiG-21F

Indian tail markings

BC821-

Black

Saffron
White
Green

Plan view, MiG-21F

Detail 'Atoll' rocket and rail

Dk. Grey

White
Red
Blue

Dk. Grey

'C' & 'D'
4

'C' & 'D'
5

Czech and Indian insignia

Red
Black edge
White

Green
White
Saffron

Note handed colours
on opposite wing

Scale
0 1 2 3 4 5 6 7 8 ft
0   1   2m

Underplan, MiG-21F ▼

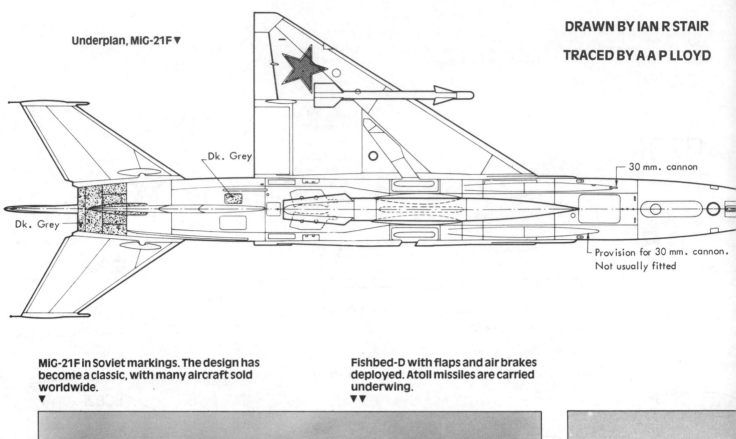

DRAWN BY IAN R STAIR

TRACED BY A A P LLOYD

Dk. Grey

Dk. Grey

30 mm. cannon

Provision for 30 mm. cannon.
Not usually fitted

MiG-21F in Soviet markings. The design has become a classic, with many aircraft sold worldwide.
▼

Fishbed-D with flaps and air brakes deployed. Atoll missiles are carried underwing.
▼▼

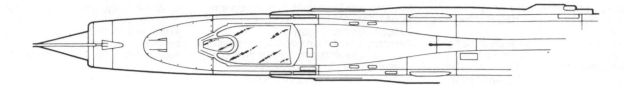

▲
Scrap plan view, MiG-21PF

Scrap underplan, MiG-21PF
▼

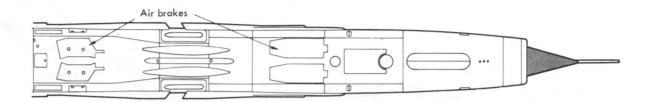

Air brakes

Polish Air Force MiG-21PF, showing enlarged spine and relocated pitot tube.
▼

Vickers VC10 C Mk 1

Country of origin: Great Britain.
Type: Long-range land-based transport aircraft.
Dimensions: Wing span 146ft 2in *44.55m*; length 158ft 8in *48.36m*; height 39ft 6in *12.04m*; wing area 2932 sq ft *272.39m²*.
Weights: Empty 323,000lb *146,485kg*.

Powerplant: Four Rolls-Royce Conway RCo42/2 Mk 540 turbojets each of 20,250lb *9184kg* thrust.
Performance: Maximum speed (cruise) 610mph *980kph* (Mach 0.89) at 26,000ft *7925m*; initial climb rate 2750ft/min *840m/min*; service ceiling 45,000ft

13,720m; range (maximum payload) 5500 miles *8850km*.
Armament: None.
Service: First flight (civil VC-10) 29 June 1962, (C Mk 1) 26 November 1965.

▲
The ninth VC10, G-ARVI, in BOAC colours, takes off from the Vickers (BAC) airfield at Weybridge, 20 December 1963.

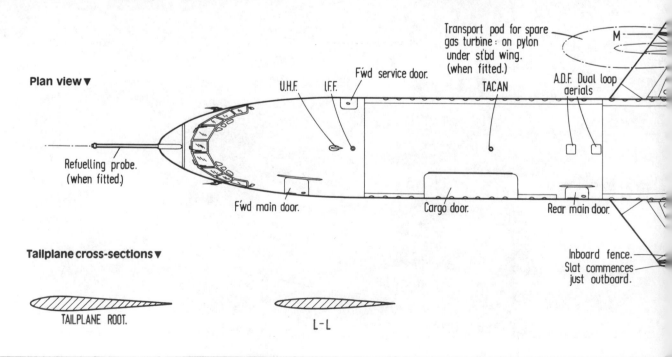

Plan view ▼

Refuelling probe. (when fitted.)

U.H.F.   I.F.F.   F'wd service door.

Transport pod for spare gas turbine: on pylon under st'bd wing. (when fitted.)

TACAN

A.D.F. Dual loop aerials

M—

F'wd main door.   Cargo door.   Rear main door.

Inboard fence.
Slat commences just outboard.

Tailplane cross-sections ▼

TAILPLANE ROOT.

L-L

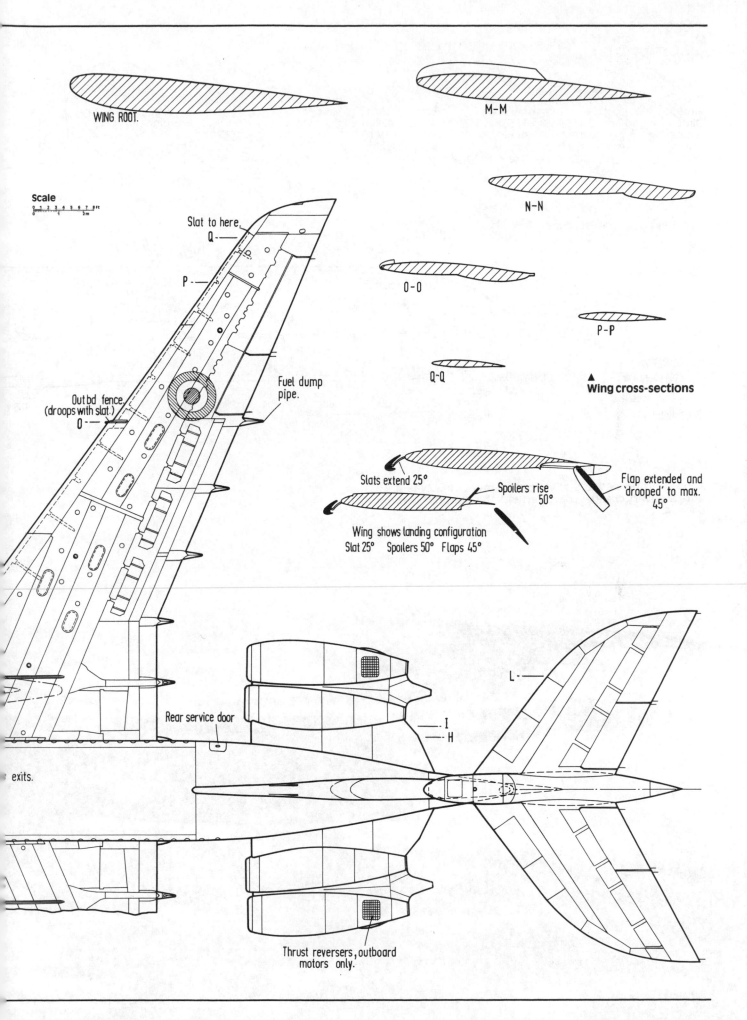

WING ROOT.

M–M

N–N

O–O

P–P

Q–Q

Wing cross-sections

Scale

Slat to here.
Q –

P –

Out bd fence.
(droops with slat.)
O –

Fuel dump
pipe.

Slats extend 25°

Spoilers rise
50°

Flap extended and
'drooped' to max.
45°

Wing shows landing configuration
Slat 25°   Spoilers 50°   Flaps 45°

L –

I
H

Rear service door

exits.

Thrust reversers, outboard
motors only.

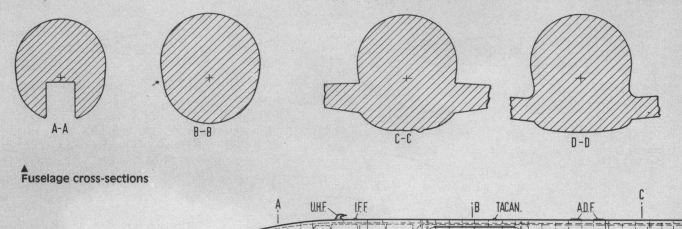

A-A   B-B   C-C   D-D

▲ Fuselage cross-sections

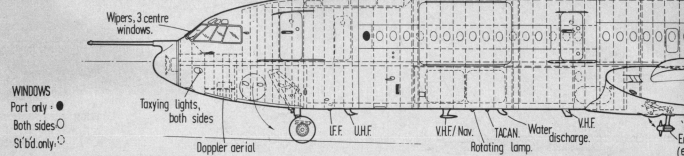

A   U.H.F.   I.F.F   ¡B   TACAN.   A.D.F.   C

Wipers, 3 centre windows.

WINDOWS
Port only : ●
Both sides: ○
St'b'd.only: ◌

Taxying lights, both sides

Doppler aerial

I.F.F.   U.H.F.

V.H.F./Nav.   TACAN.   Water discharge.   V.H.F.

Rotating lamp.

Another VC10 for BOAC, G-ARVM, photographed in July 1964. Note the livery changes compared with the aircraft shown on page 74.
▼

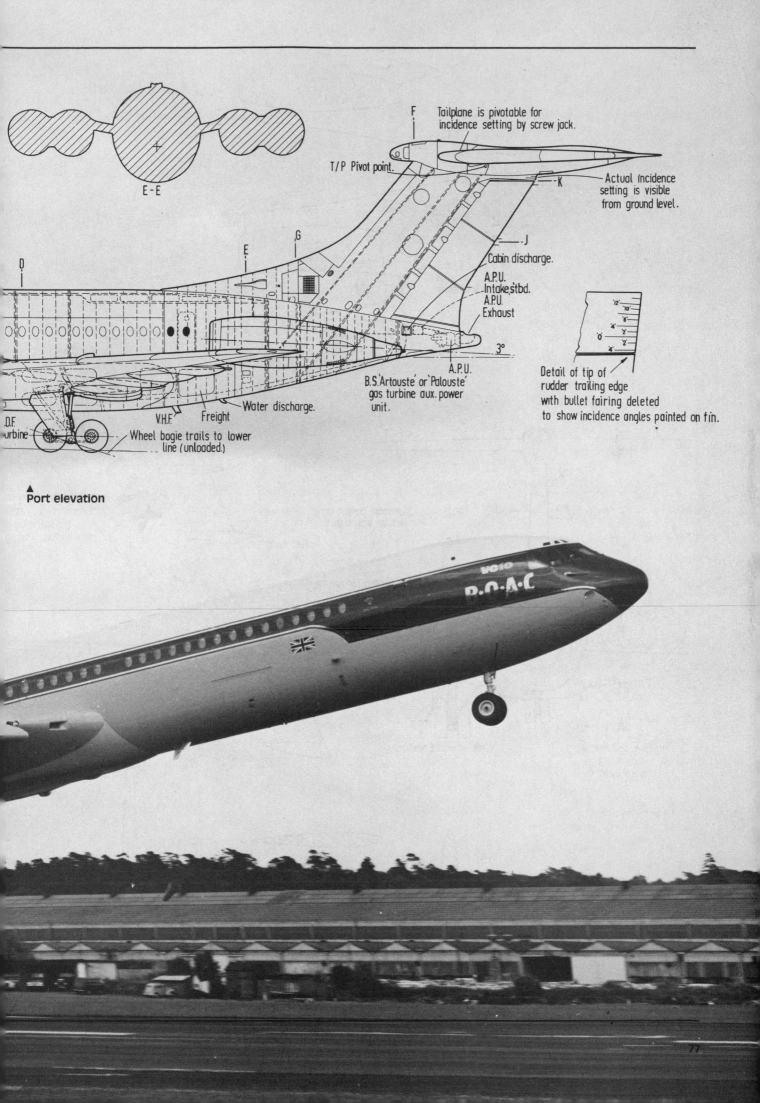

E-E

T/P Pivot point.

F

Tailplane is pivotable for
incidence setting by screw jack.

K

Actual incidence
setting is visible
from ground level.

J

Cabin discharge.

A.P.U.
Intake, stbd.
A.P.U.
Exhaust

3°

A.P.U.

B.S. 'Artouste' or 'Palouste'
gas turbine aux. power
unit.

Water discharge.

V.H.F.

Freight

D.F.
urbine

Wheel bogie trails to lower
line (unloaded.)

D

E

G

Detail of tip of
rudder trailing edge
with bullet fairing deleted
to show incidence angles painted on fin.

12'
10'
8'
6'
4'
2'
0'
2'
4'

▲
Port elevation

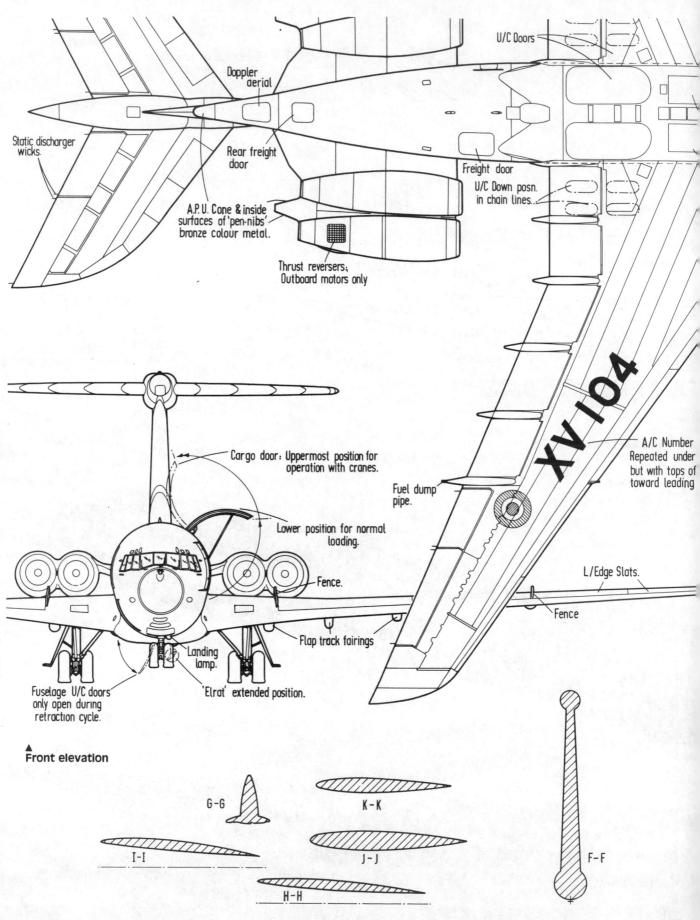

Static discharger wicks.

Doppler aerial

U/C Doors

Rear freight door

Freight door

U/C Down posn. in chain lines...

A.P.U. Cone & inside surfaces of 'pen-nibs' bronze colour metal.

Thrust reversers; Outboard motors only

XV 104

A/C Number Repeated under but with tops of toward leading

Fuel dump pipe.

Cargo door: Uppermost position for operation with cranes.

Lower position for normal loading.

Fence.

L/Edge Slats.

Fence

Flap track fairings

Landing lamp.

Fuselage U/C doors only open during retraction cycle.

'Elrat' extended position.

▲ **Front elevation**

G-G

K-K

I-I

J-J

H-H

F-F

Wing and tailplane cross-sections ▲

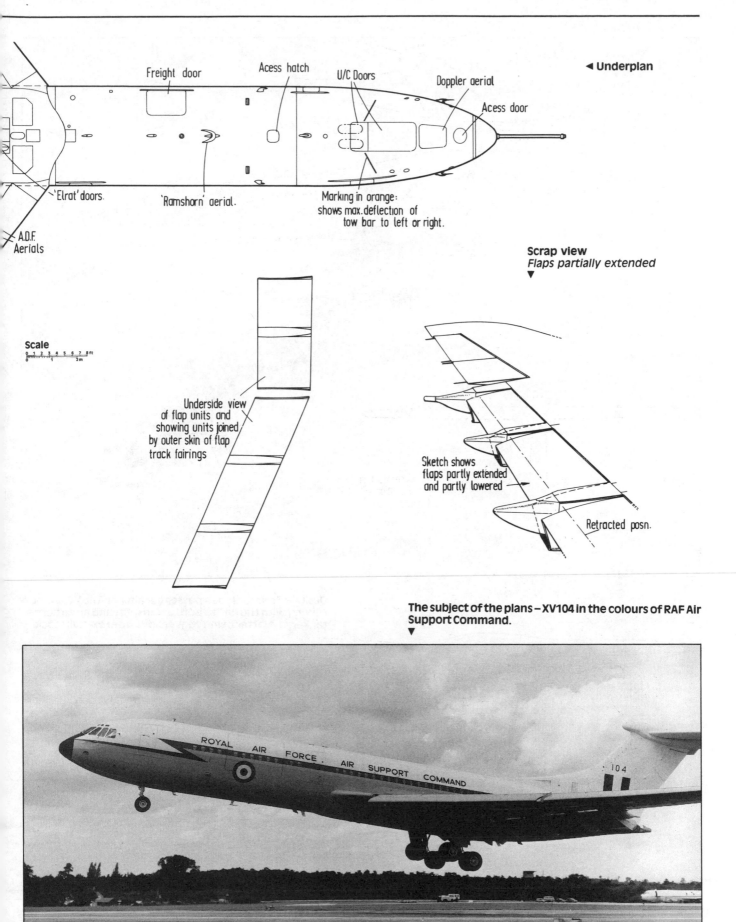

Freight door

Acess hatch

U/C Doors

Doppler aerial

Acess door

'Elrat' doors.

'Ramshorn' aerial.

Marking in orange:
shows max.deflection of
tow bar to left or right.

A.D.F.
Aerials

Scrap view
Flaps partially extended
▼

Scale
0 1 2 3 4 5 6 7 8ft
0   1   2m

Underside view
of flap units and
showing units joined
by outer skin of flap
track fairings

Sketch shows
flaps partly extended
and partly lowered

Retracted posn.

The subject of the plans – XV104 in the colours of RAF Air
Support Command.
▼

ROYAL AIR FORCE . AIR SUPPORT COMMAND

104

▲ Designed primarily as a passenger airliner, the VC10 is now serving with the RAF as both a transport and an airborne tanker, the latter being conversions from ex-civil stock.

Starboard elevation
▼

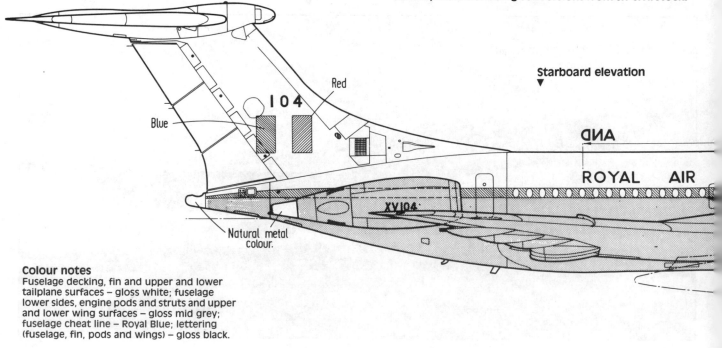

Colour notes
Fuselage decking, fin and upper and lower tailplane surfaces – gloss white; fuselage lower sides, engine pods and struts and upper and lower wing surfaces – gloss mid grey; fuselage cheat line – Royal Blue; lettering (fuselage, fin, pods and wings) – gloss black.

▲
Current RAF VC10 transports retain the original-style livery, although tankers are painted in Hemp and Light Aircraft Grey camouflage.

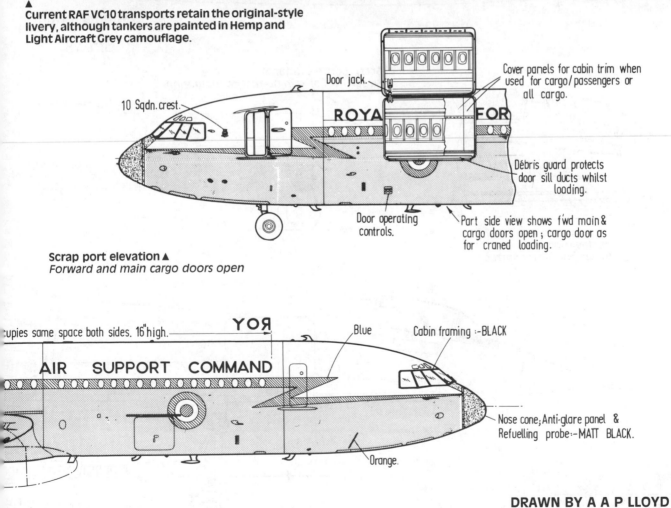

10 Sqdn. crest.

Door jack.

Cover panels for cabin trim when used for cargo/passengers or all cargo.

ROYA FOR

Débris guard protects door sill ducts whilst loading.

Door operating controls.

Part side view shows f'wd main & cargo doors open; cargo door as for craned loading.

Scrap port elevation ▲
Forward and main cargo doors open

...cupies same space both sides. 16"high.

Blue

Cabin framing :-BLACK

AIR SUPPORT COMMAND

Nose cone; Anti-glare panel & Refuelling probe:-MATT BLACK.

Orange.

DRAWN BY A A P LLOYD

BAC TSR2

Country of origin: Great Britain.
Type: Two-seat, land-based tactical bomber and reconnaissance aircraft.
Dimensions: Wing span 37ft 0in *11.28m*;

length 89ft 0in *27.13m*; height 24ft 0in *7.32m*.
Powerplant: Two Bristol Siddeley Olympus 22R afterburning turbojets

each of 33,000lb *14,966kg* thrust.
Performance: Maximum speed over Mach 2.0 at altitude.
Service: First flight 27 September 1964.

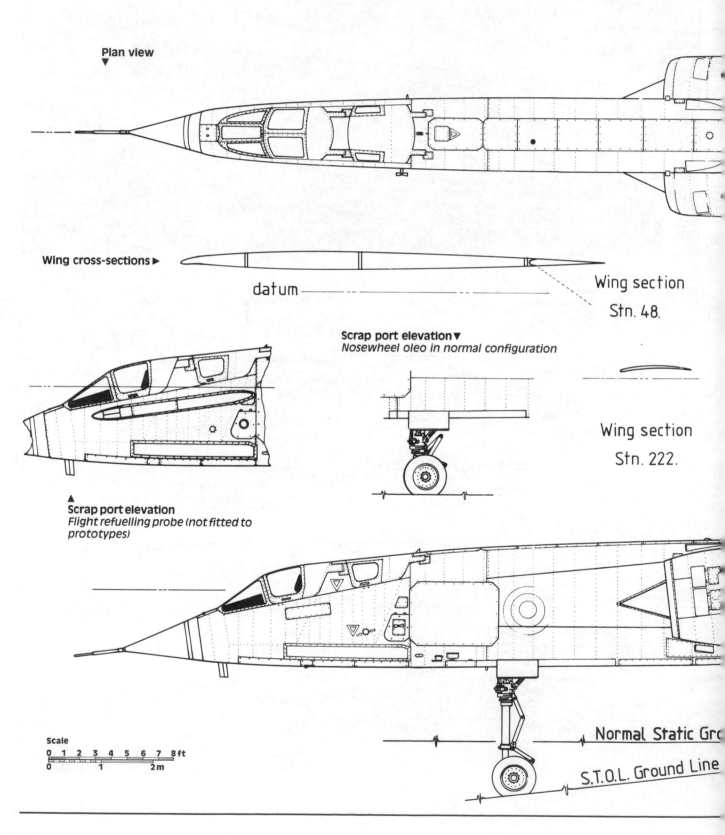

Plan view ▼

Wing cross-sections ▶

datum

Wing section Stn. 48.

Wing section Stn. 222.

Scrap port elevation ▼
Nosewheel oleo in normal configuration

▲
Scrap port elevation
Flight refuelling probe (not fitted to prototypes)

Normal Static Gr

S.T.O.L. Ground Line

Scale
0 1 2 3 4 5 6 7 8 ft
0 1 2m

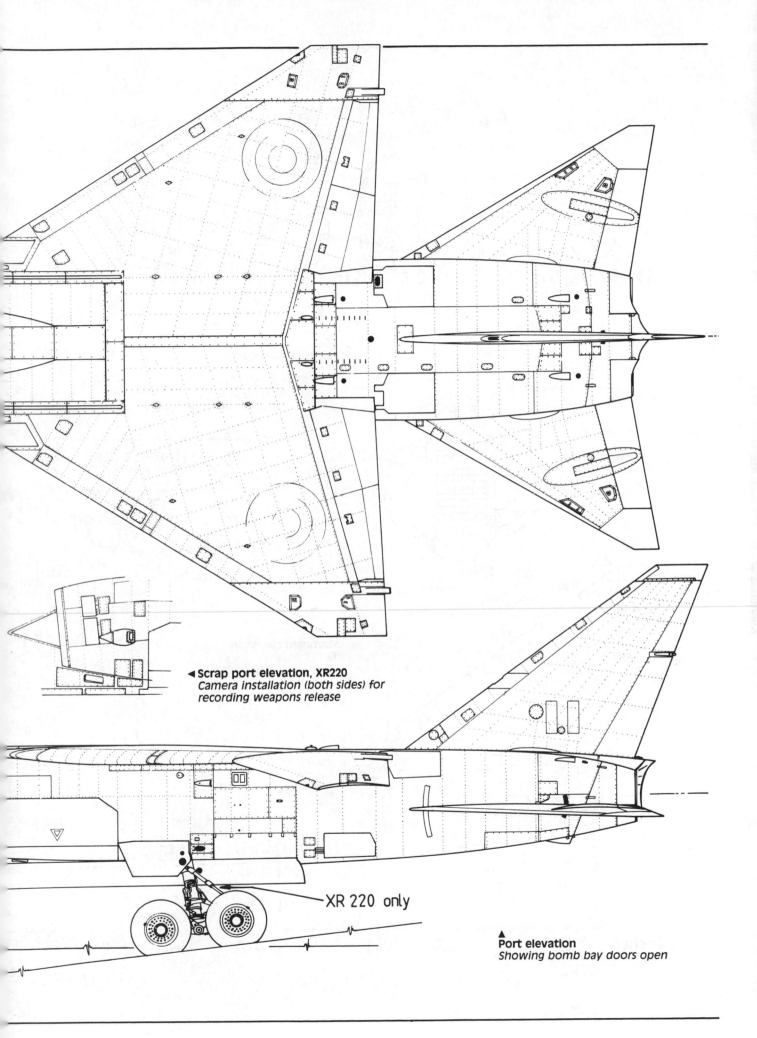

◄ **Scrap port elevation, XR220**
Camera installation (both sides) for recording weapons release

XR 220 only

▲
Port elevation
Showing bomb bay doors open

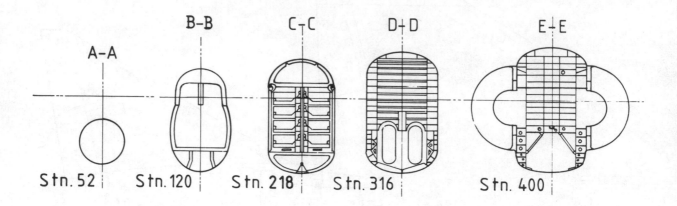

A–A B–B C–C D÷D E÷E
Stn. 52 Stn. 120 Stn. 218 Stn. 316 Stn. 400

▲ Fuselage cross-sections

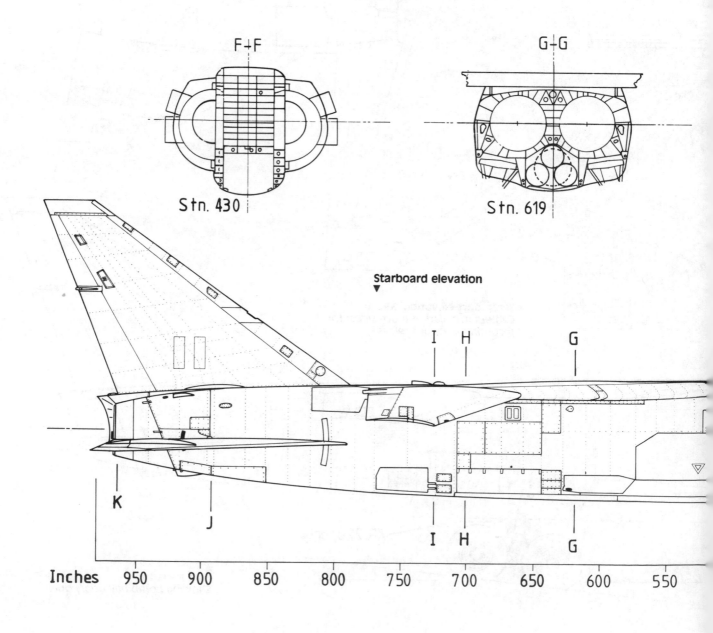

F÷F
Stn. 430

G÷G
Stn. 619

Starboard elevation
▼

I H G

K

J

I H G

Inches 950 900 850 800 750 700 650 600 550

▲
The TSR2, replacement for the Canberra, was cancelled in 1965, causing the biggest controversy in postwar British military aviation affairs.

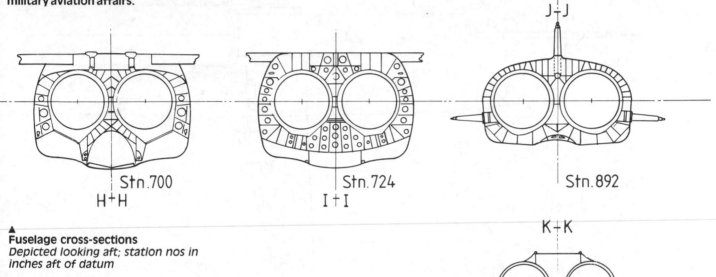

Stn.700
H+H

Stn.724
I+I

Stn.892

J–J

▲
Fuselage cross-sections
Depicted looking aft; station nos in inches aft of datum

K+K

Stn.965

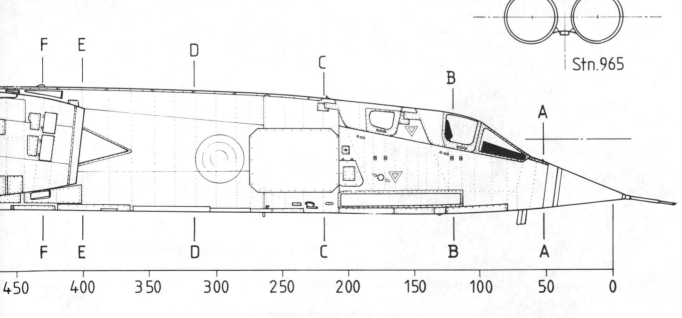

| F | E | D | C | B | A |

| F | E | D | C | B | A |

450   400   350   300   250   200   150   100   50   0

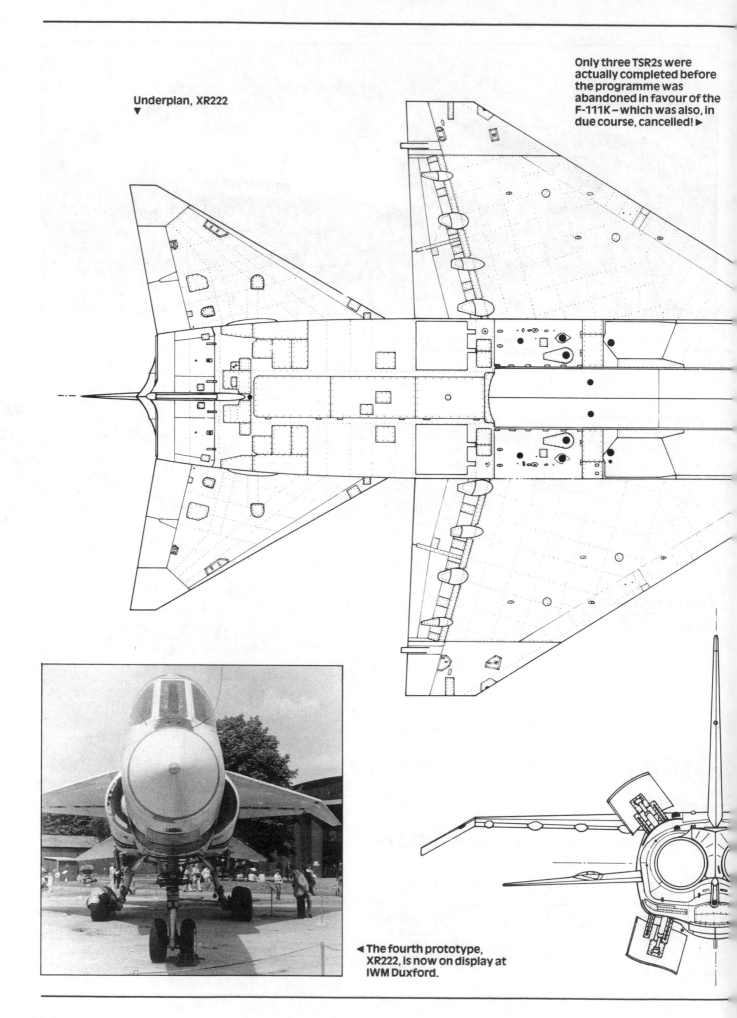

Underplan, XR222
▼

Only three TSR2s were
actually completed before
the programme was
abandoned in favour of the
F-111K – which was also, in
due course, cancelled! ▶

◀ The fourth prototype,
XR222, is now on display at
IWM Duxford.

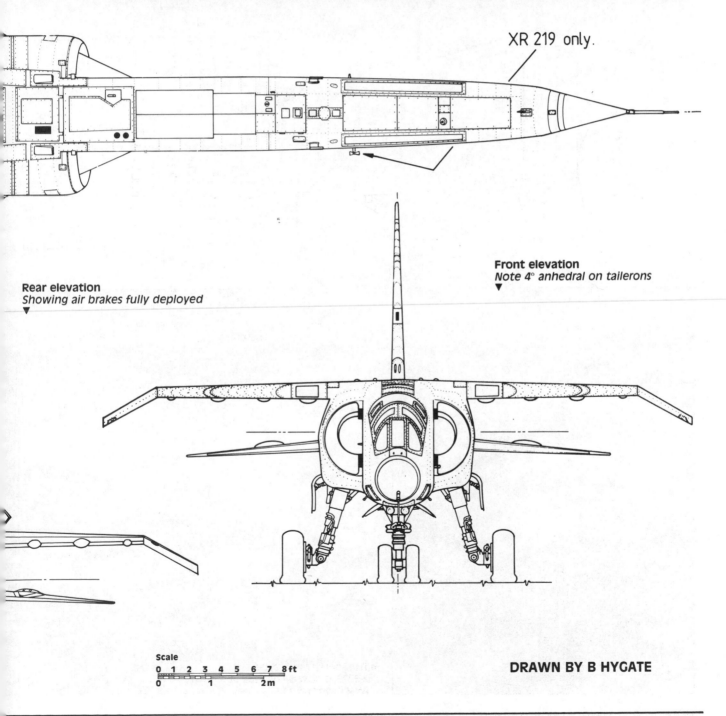

XR 219 only.

Rear elevation
Showing air brakes fully deployed
▼

Front elevation
Note 4° anhedral on tailerons
▼

Scale
0 1 2 3 4 5 6 7 8 ft
0   1   2 m

DRAWN BY B HYGATE

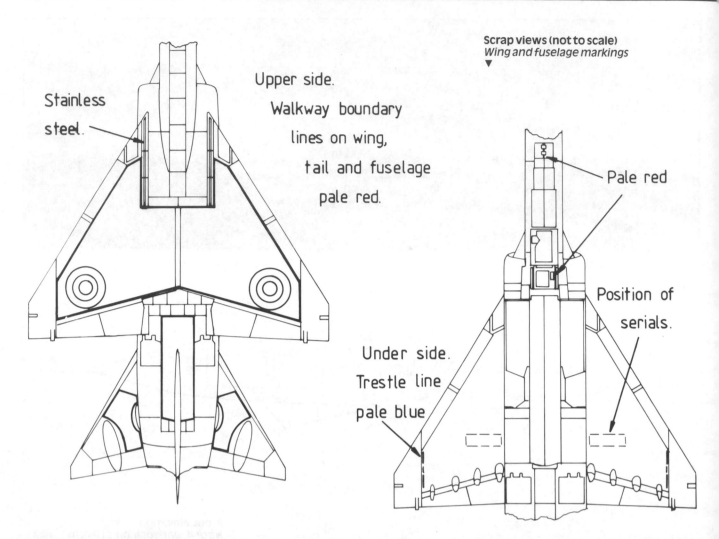

Stainless steel.

Upper side.
Walkway boundary
lines on wing,
tail and fuselage
pale red.

Pale red

Position of serials.

Under side.
Trestle line
pale blue

Scrap views
Layout of engine intake ducting and cross-section (constant section aft of 'Z')
▼

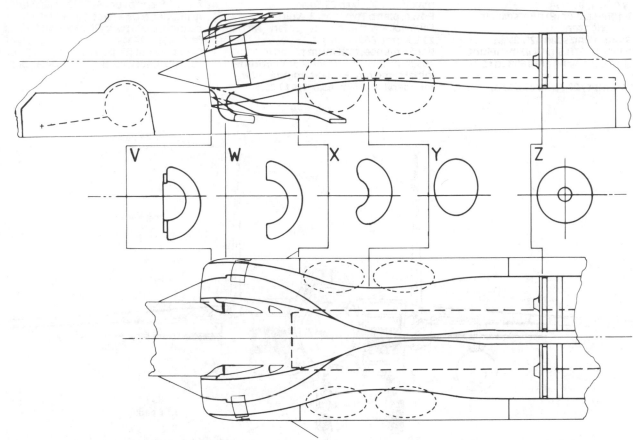

V   W   X   Y   Z

Scrap views ▶
Typical plate aerial

Notes

Plate aerials on wing tips, fin and tail surfaces varied with prototype; those shown are as fitted to XR222. Larger main, and nose, undercarriage doors sequenced closed after undercarriage extension. Panel details varied slightly with prototype. Provision for underwing pylons at wing stations 120 and 155, but pylons never fitted to prototypes.

Colour notes

Overall acrylic white to Specification DTD900/4740, except for dielectric panels and nose cone, polished stainless steel tail cone, upper wing panels and leading edges of flap undersurfaces. All markings in pale red or blue to same Specification; serials on wing undersides and rear fuselage sides in pale blue, all with 16in characters.

◀ Rear view shows the huge Olympus tailpipes and unusual taileron configuration. Slab fin was pivoted to act as a rudder.

McDonnell Douglas F-15A and B Eagle

Country of origin: USA.
Type: Single-seat or (B) two-seat air superiority fighter.
Dimensions: Wing span 42ft 9¾in *13.05m*; length 63ft 9in *19.43m*; height 18ft 5½in *5.63m*; wing area 608 sq ft *56.48m²*.
Weights: Empty 27,381lb *12,418kg*;

maximum 56,000lb *25,397kg*.
Powerplant: Two Pratt & Whitney F100-100 afterburning turbofans each of 23,950lb *10,860kg* thrust.
Performance: Maximum speed (clean) 1650mph *2655kph* (Mach 2.5) at altitude; initial climb rate 55,000ft/min *16,760m/min*; service ceiling 63,000ft *19,200m*;

range (ferry) over 2500 miles *4025km*.
Armament: One fixed 20mm M61A1 cannon, plus (typically) four AIM-7 and four AIM-9 AAMs.
Service: First flight (A) 27 July 1972, (B) 7 July 1973; service entry 14 November 1974.

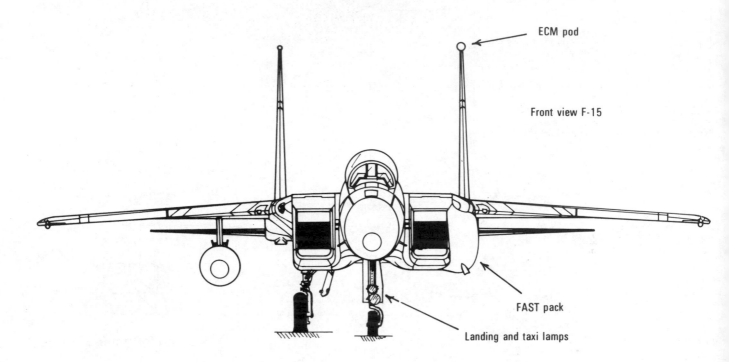

ECM pod

Front view F-15

FAST pack

Landing and taxi lamps

Front elevation, F-15A

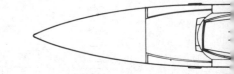

F-15A of the 555th TFS, 405th TTW, based at Luke AFB in Arizona, with centreline tank but no missiles. The aircraft carries the standard 36320/36375 grey camouflage finish.

▲
A 325th TTW F-15A. Note, in this and the previous photo, the main intakes nodding downwards, controlling the airflow to the engines.

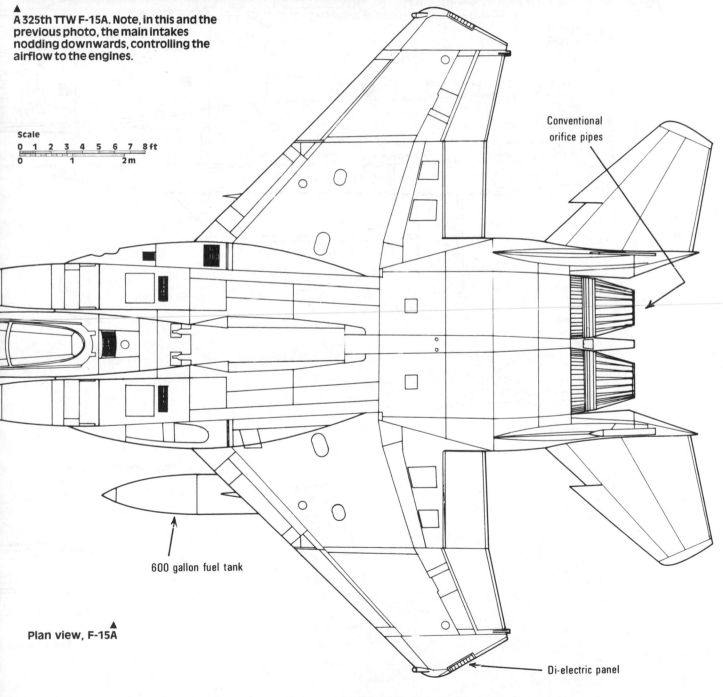

Scale

0 1 2 3 4 5 6 7 8 ft
0   1   2 m

Conventional orifice pipes

600 gallon fuel tank

Di-electric panel

Plan view, F-15A ▲

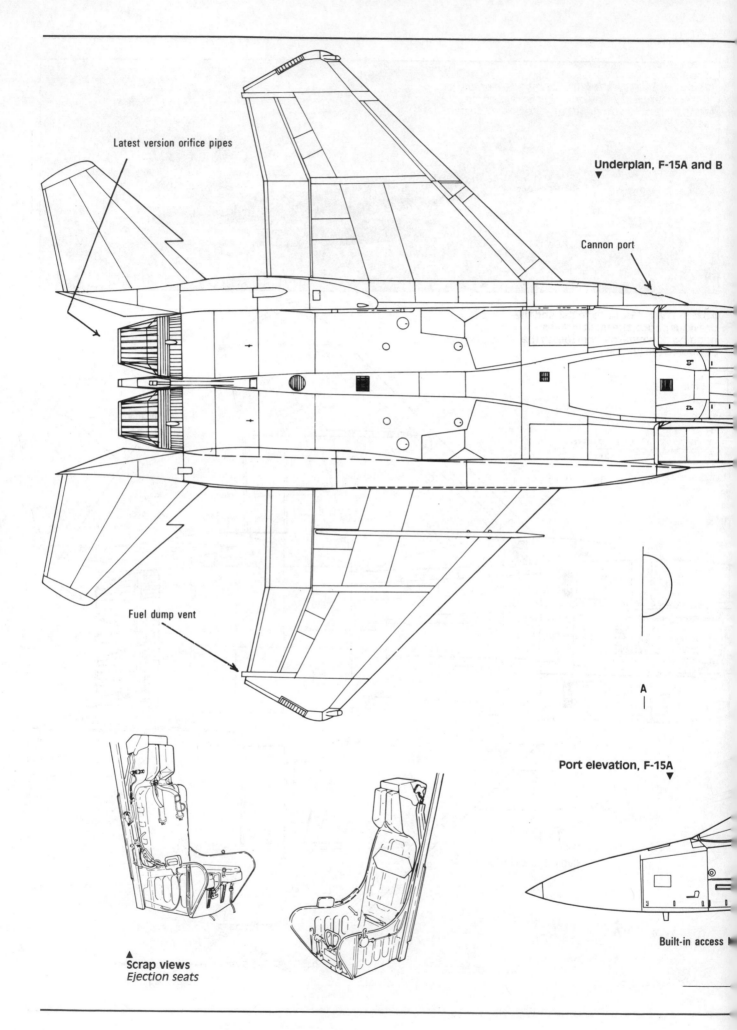

Latest version orifice pipes

Underplan, F-15A and B
▼

Cannon port

Fuel dump vent

A

Port elevation, F-15A
▼

Built-in access

▲
Scrap views
Ejection seats

The Eagle's missile armament comprises four AIM-7s and four AIM-9s in the layout shown here, the latter weapons carried on shoulder rails on the wing pylons, allowing fuel tanks to be carried here as well if desired.▶

Scale
0 1 2 3 4 5 6 7 8 ft
0   1   2 m

Fuselage cross-sections, F-15A
▼

Dotted lines show
FAST pack

C   D   E   F

ECM pod

White lamp

Airbrake extended, strake
only used on first block F-15As

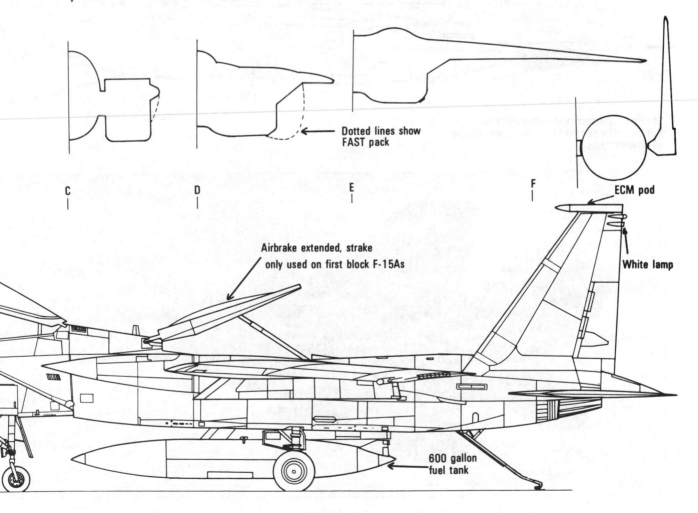

600 gallon
fuel tank

The first F-15E Strike Eagle proper, with FAST packs and LANTIRN pods on the intakes. This version is scheduled to enter service with the USAF in 1988–89 as its Dual Role Fighter. ▶

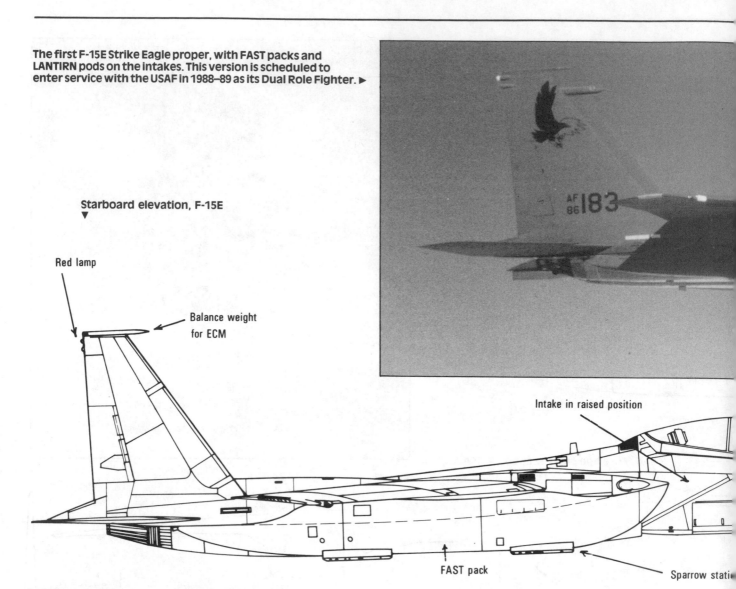

Starboard elevation, F-15E
▼

Red lamp

Balance weight for ECM

Intake in raised position

FAST pack

Sparrow stati…

Strike Eagle demonstrator aircraft, actually the second two-seat prototype in new clothes.
▼

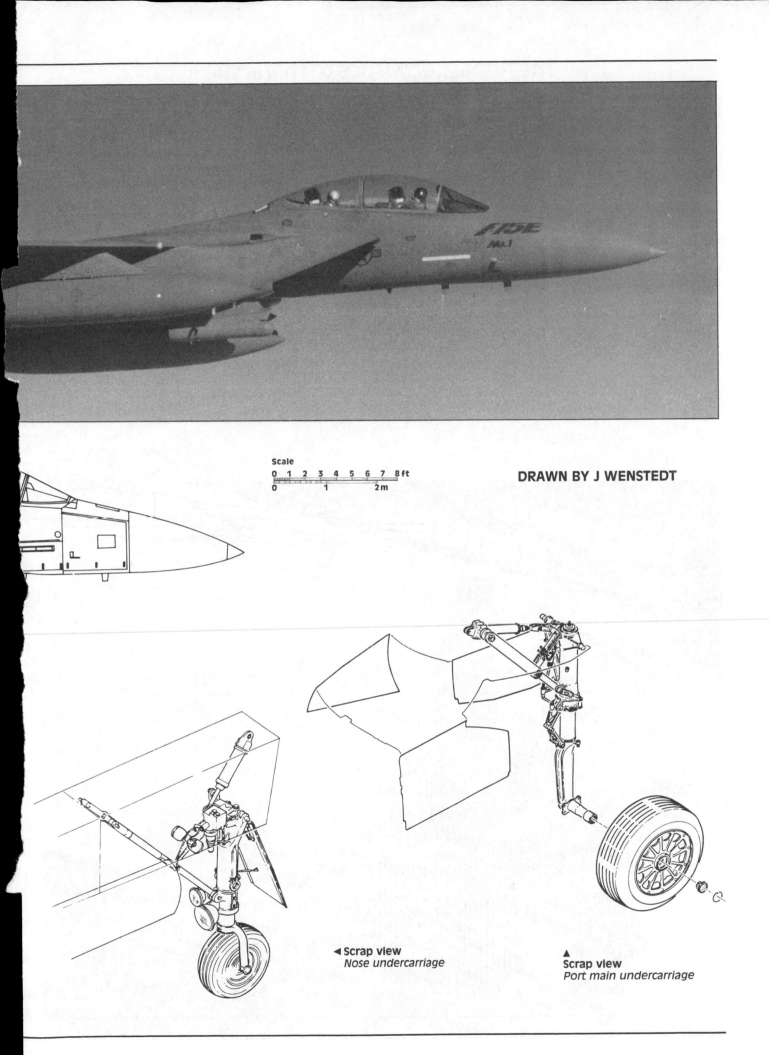

Scale

0 1 2 3 4 5 6 7 8 ft

0 1 2m

DRAWN BY J WENSTEDT

◄ **Scrap view**
Nose undercarriage

▲
Scrap view
Port main undercarriage

The Publisher wishes to thank the
following draughtsmen whose drawings
appear in this volume

ARTHUR BENTLEY	J F HENDERSON
A H BUTLER	B HYGATE
D H COOKSEY	PAT LLOYD
PETER G COOKSLEY	R G MOULTON
GEORGE CULL	IAN R STAIR
J R ENOCH	J WENSTEDT

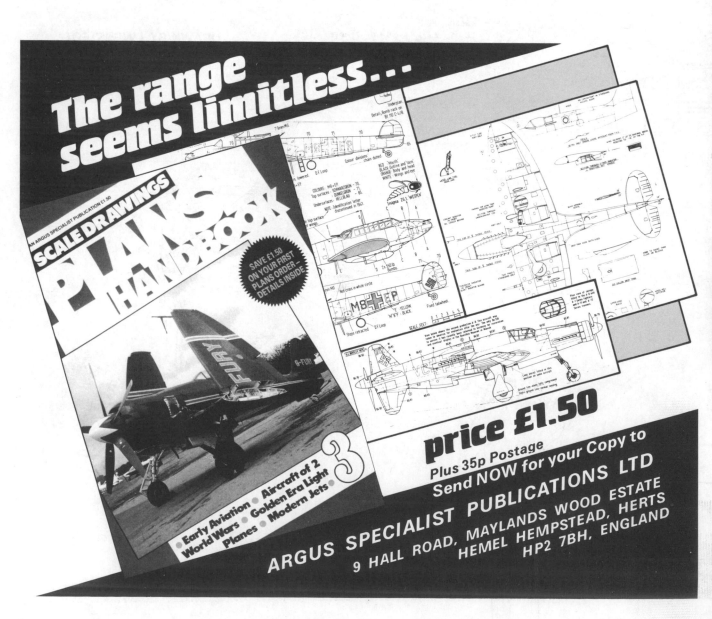